A Short Account of
Greek Philosophy
from Thales to Epicurus

A Short Account of
Greek Philosophy
from Thales to Epicurus

G. F. PARKER

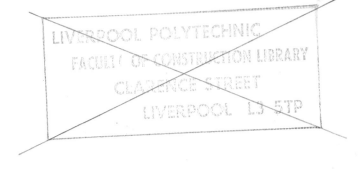

Edward Arnold (Publishers) Ltd

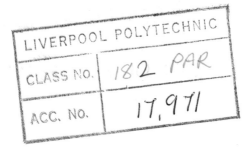
Printed in Great Britain by
Robert Cunningham and Sons Ltd, Alva

Preface

Each year sees an increased number of students entering the upper forms of our schools, our colleges and our universities. Most are not only studying some subject or subjects in depth but are also following a course of General or Liberal Studies. Many have no first-hand or formal acquaintance with Classical thought and are constantly meeting references to Greek philosophers and common philosophical terms. They are also discovering that, however important and interesting their particular subjects, there is a great deal of truth in the words of Sir Karl Popper: 'We are not students of some subject matter but students of problems. And problems cut right across the borders of any subject matter or discipline.' The history of man's thought recognises no arbitrarily erected barriers.

There are, too, the 'students' who are not formally enrolled in any educational establishment and who are travelling each year to Greece in unprecedented numbers to explore at first hand the more palpable remains of Classical and pre-Classical ages. Excellent guide books for the traveller are already numerous and continue to multiply. But however good the guide books, one cannot easily capture the spirit of, say, Heracleitus or Democritus or Plato as one wanders round an ancient temple site or modern museum.

It has been my intention to provide information and some common ground for students, whatever their subjects of study or interests may be. Plato and Aristotle cannot be ignored; nor can they be understood except in relation to their times and their predecessors, the pre-Socratic philosophers. And the pre-Socratics are not merely important; they are intellectually exciting and have a certain affinity with our present age.

I should like to express my thanks to my colleague, Mr J. S. Blandford, who suggested the inclusion of Greek Philosophy in Sixth Form General Studies and prompted me to put the contents of this course into more permanent form, and to my wife for her encouragement and help, particularly in compiling the index.

v

Contents

Chapter		Page
I	Introduction. The 'Two Cultures' – an Educational and Social Problem	1
II	Roots in the Great Rivers	8
III	The Ionians: Thales, Anaximander and Anaximenes	17
IV	Pythagoras: Mathematics and Mysticism	25
V	Pythagoras and Orpheus	32
VI	Heracleitus of Ephesus	36
VII	Parmenides and Zeno of Elea	43
VIII	Empedocles and Anaxagoras: Signposts to the Atom Country	52
IX	The Atomists	62
X	Athens – Sparta – City States	73
XI	Socrates	85
XII	Plato (1). The Theory	90
XIII	Plato (2). *The Republic*	105
XIV	Plato (3). *The Laws*	117
XV	Aristotle (1). The Man and his Works	132
XVI	Aristotle (2). His Views of Nature	139
XVII	Aristotle (3). *The Ethics* and *The Politics*	151
XVIII	Aristotle (4). His Position in History	162
XIX	Hellenism and Alexandria	172
XX	Conclusion	181
Index		189

Acknowledgments

We would like to thank the following for permission for extracts used in this book:

Laurence Pollinger Limited and Holt, Rinehart & Winston, Inc. for *Why Wait for Science?* by Robert Frost; Macmillan & Co. Ltd. and the Macmillan Co. of New York for *Among School Children* by W. B. Yeats; Penguin Books Ltd. for extracts from *The Iliad*, Homer, translated by E. V. Rieu, *The Odyssey*, Homer, translated by E. V. Rieu, *The Nature of the Universe*, Lucretius, translated by R. E. Latham, *The Last Days of Socrates*, Plato, translated by Hugh Tredennick, *Protagoras and Meno*, Plato, translated by W. K. C. Guthrie, *The Ethics*, Aristotle, translated by J. A. Thomson, *The Politics*, Aristotle, translated by T. A. Sinclair; Faber & Faber Ltd. and University of Chicago Press for extracts from *A Portrait of Aristotle* by Marjorie Grene; Dent & Sons Ltd. and E. P. Dutton & Co. Inc. for an extract from *Parmenides and Other Dialoges*, translated by John Warrington; The Bodley Head Ltd. for extracts from *The Peloponnesian War*, Thucydides, translated by Rex Warner.

A Table of Dates

Chief figures	Place(s) associated with	Dates or Date in Prime
Thales	Miletus	585
Anaximander	Miletus	560
Anaximenes	Miletus	546
Pythagoras	Samos, Croton	530
Heracleitus	Ephesus	500
Parmenides	Elea	475
Zeno	Elea	450
Anaxagoras	Athens	460
Empedocles	Acragas	450
Leucippus	Abdera? Miletus?	430
Democritus	Abdera	420
Socrates	Athens	469-399
Plato	Athens	427-347
Aristotle	Athens	384-322
Alexander	Macedon, Asia, Alexandria	356-323
Diogenes	Corinth, Athens	412-323
Epicurus	Athens	341-270
Zeno	Athens	336-264
Archimedes	Syracuse	287-212
Lucretius	Rome	98-55

NOTE: *all dates are B.C.*

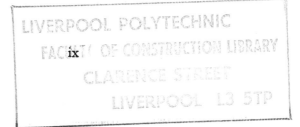
ix

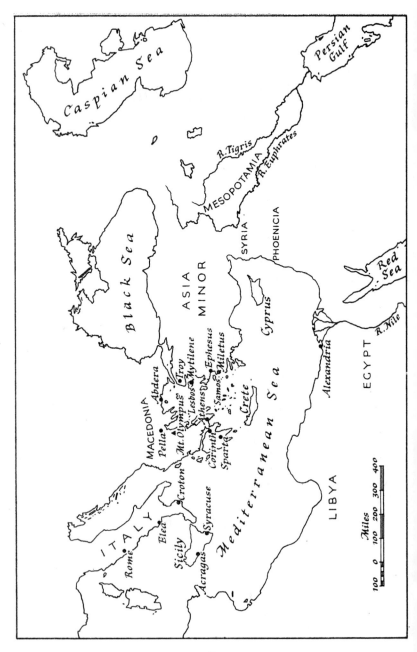

CHAPTER I

Introduction

We shall not cease from exploration
And the end of all our exploring
Will be to arrive where we started
And know the place for the first time.

T. S. ELIOT: *Four Quartets*

That there is nothing new under the sun is simply not true. Anyone visiting the London Planetarium will find in the foyer a veritable travel guide – not of our railways, for we seem already to have passed out of the railway era – but of ballistics, of space-craft and man-made moons. A highly complicated camera, propelled from the earth by man, has circled and photographed the far side of the moon. Men walk in space. Here we have something new. New knowledge, new techniques, new arrangements of earth-old ingredients and, above all, new approaches to old problems.

But every novel achievement stems from a long, continuous line of challenge reaching back from the present through earlier civilisations to the primitive past. The story of man's interest in the moon offers a ready example. Primitive man, the hunter and the planter, used the moon as his time-piece. Anaxagoras, the philosopher, was expelled from Athens because, amongst other things, he said that the moon was no more than a disc of incandescent rock. Plato and Aristotle restored it to its status of divinity. Galileo with his newly invented telescope saw and said that the face of the goddess was pock-marked, thereby outraging her divinity and questioning her perfection. A certain Dr John Wilkins, one of the founders of the Royal Society, used to exercise his imagination on schemes for man's flight to the moon. And now, although it may not be

... an easy leap
to pluck bright honour from the pale-faced moon,
there is little doubt that the leap will be made – provided the techni-

cally advanced nations employ their ballistics for exploration rather than extermination.

Similarly, a continuous thread runs through the history of thought; every advance is coupled in some way or other to preceding events or groups of events and, as it were, grows out of them. So that in considering Greek Philosophy from the vantage point of the twentieth century, there is a sense in which it is valuable to imagine, not that we are looking at an early as opposed to a modern civilisation, but that we are looking at early and advanced stages of the same problems, earlier and later answers to the same questions. And what are these questions? Of what is this universe made? Can the universe with all its manifold variety of creatures and materials be reduced to a single, basic, underlying 'stuff'? Is there any purpose in the universe and, if so, what is it? Can wisdom and power ever reside in the same people?

At this point in history another old problem is presenting itself with new force and in a new way: a generation of scientists is being bred whose work and language are fast becoming incomprehensible to those who, while not scientifically trained, are otherwise well educated. We are fast moving towards the point where the divergence will be of serious magnitude and where the graphic anecdote recorded by Graves and Hodge about Einstein may be relevant to an alarming degree. Einstein, on being asked by an American lady to explain his theory of relativity simply in a few words replied:

> My dear Lady: A blind man was walking with a friend down a hot and dusty road. His friend said:
> O for a nice drink of milk!
> Drink I know, but what is this milk you speak of?
> A white liquid.
> Liquid I know, but what is white?
> White is the colour of a swan's feathers.
> Feathers I know, but what is a swan?
> A bird with a crooked neck.
> Neck I know, but what is crooked?
> The exasperated friend seized the blind man's arm and extended it at full length. 'That is straight', he exclaimed, and then, bending it at the elbow, 'This is crooked.'
> 'Ah!' cried the delighted blind man, '*Now* I understand what milk is.'[1]

[1] *The Long Week-end* (Faber).

This divergence tends to create suspicion between artist and scientist. The artist feels that the tide is running for the scientist and is tempted to distrust him or ignore him altogether. W. B. Yeats is an outstanding example of the artist turning his back on science. He records his feelings of hatred for Tyndall and Huxley. And when Mme Blavatsky kept the poet waiting in the hall of her London house because she thought it was another man who would probably try to persuade her that the earth was flat, one is sometimes tempted to wonder if there really was any other man.

The American poet, Robert Frost, rather less given to riding the clouds than Yeats, at least considers the scientist and his work and gently chides him like an understanding father:

> Sarcastic Science she would like to know,
> In her complacent ministry of fear,
> How we propose to get away from here
> When she has made things so we have to go
> Or be wiped out. Will she be asked to show
> Us how by rocket we may hope to steer
> To some star off there say a half light-year
> Through temperature of absolute zero?
> Why wait for Science to supply the how
> When any amateur can tell it now?
> The way to go away should be the same
> As fifty million years ago we came –
> If anyone remembers how that was.
> I have a theory, but it hardly does.[1]

The scientist, for his part, grows impatient with and mistrusts much of the century's poetry, and sometimes with much greater justification than his illustrious ancestor, Newton, who exclaimed that in his opinion poetry was a kind of ingenious nonsense. Because of this estrangement between Art and Science there is an ever increasing danger that the scientist may underestimate the emotional experience in the widest sense and that the artist, whose peculiar role it is to enrich emotional life, may be unable to play his part adequately.

We are, after all, living through an explosive period of scientific discovery and intellectual adventure unparallelled in history. And the fact that much of the knowledge gained may be directed towards evil ends by those in whose hands economic and political power lies,

[1] *Why wait for Science?*

does not necessarily diminish the reasonable and legitimate excitement which new discoveries produce. In Brecht's play when Galileo is in a ferment of excitement on having discovered the moons of the planet, Jupiter, his assistant, Sagredo cries: 'Galileo, calm yourself!' But Galileo, knowing well that

> ... any action
> is a step to the block, to the fire,
> down the sea's throat

merely shouts back:

> Sagredo, show some excitement yourself!

Alexander Pope considering the vistas opened up by the science of his day displays a similar excited interest:

> Th' increasing prospects tire our wand'ring eyes,
> Hills peep o'er hills, and Alps on Alps arise.

This does not mean, of course, that we can equate knowledge with wisdom or identify interplanetary probes and pigmented polymers with progress. But knowledge may lead to wisdom, and knowledge is indivisible. Exploration too is indivisible, whether it is carried out with the assistance of a Muse or a microscope. (Indeed, for the Greeks, Ourania who presided over the study of astronomy was numbered among the Muses.) We have to bear in mind that Science, adrift from its moorings in humanism and history, can become a ravening monster, while the Arts, oblivious of new areas of reality revealed by Science, can become as arid as the deserts of the moon.

The content and structure of our education – in England at any rate – creates and aggravates the problem of the 'two cultures'. There are, of course, many who claim that no such problem exists or that 'culture' is too subjective a concept to admit of general definition. This point of view, however, is rather reminiscent of Mark Twain's observation on the Homeric Problem: 'It has now been discovered that the Iliad and the Odyssey were not written by Homer but by another author of the same name!' Our educational system tends to force students into separate moulds, and subsequent types of employment effectively set a seal on each mould so that – apart from exceptional cases – communication between the two ceases. Our universities demand candidates who can express competently what they know in their specialist subjects and who know something worth expressing in wider fields. But they demand of school-leavers a standard of specialist knowledge such as to preclude the possibility of exploration in those wider fields.

Some forces have come into view on the educational horizon which are launching a counter-attack on our deeply entrenched system. The Universities of North Staffordshire and Sussex, for example, have made a breach and the movement known as the Agreement to Broaden the Curriculum, which has won the support of some hundreds of headmasters, will widen it. The Crowther Report on Education in England from fifteen to eighteen makes an eloquent plea for the sixth-form members of the nation's schools to be 'literate' and 'numerate' in the widest senses of the words. Educationists and humanists are becoming aware of the significance for us of the ancient legend of Pyramus and Thisbe. They died, not by the jaws of the devouring monster, but each by a self-inflicted wound – for lack of communication.

The study of Greek Philosophy forms one of a number of common platforms on which those who wish to be both literate and numerate can meet. Greek civilisation is the common source from which the divergent streams of art and science flow down to us. It is reasonable to suppose that the student of mathematics and science may have a deeper understanding of his own discipline through an acquaintance with Greek thought from Thales to Archimedes. It is equally reasonable to claim that the 'Proud Stones of Greece' are embedded in our language and literature just as calcium is embedded in our bones. Consider, for example, these lines from a representative poem of one of the foremost poets of the century:

> Plato thought nature but a spume that plays
> Upon a ghostly paradigm of things;
> Solider Aristotle played the taws
> Upon the bottom of a king of kings.
> World-famous golden-thighed Pythagoras
> Fingered upon a fiddle-stick or strings
> What a star sang and careless Muses heard.[1]

No inflated claims should be made for any intrinsic virtue in knowing these retrospective allusions. The passage is simply one of innumer-

[1] Yeats: *Among School Children.*

able possible examples in support of the present argument, and we shall meet it again.

Education, however, is a wider and more urgent business than the formal activities of school, college and university. Paradoxically, at a time in world history when man can travel with the speed of sound and communicate with the speed of light, he is still perilously prone to self-centred and parochial ways of thought. To enlarge our time-scale by reviewing a civilisation more remote from us in time can be a valuable corrective and can assist us towards a more objective and far-sighted point of view where contemporary problems are concerned.

The Greeks believed – very rightly – that the asking of a question was the beginning of education. We might go a step further and say that the presenting of a paradox invariably stimulates a question. History and literature present us with an unending pageant of paradox, a curiously tangled chain of contradiction. Why, for example, was Socrates at one moment declared by the Delphic Oracle to be the wisest man in Greece and at another arraigned by his fellow citizens as an evil influence and executed because they won their case? If Aristotle, a truly great scholar, believed with all his intellect that wisdom invariably lay in the choice of the mean of two extremes, and Blake, a truly great poet, believed with all his heart that 'the road of excess leads to the palace of wisdom', where is truth to be found? It is not merely that the poet disagrees with the philosopher, for there is equal disagreement between the poets. Alexander Pope, finding his inspiration in the Classical World, writes:

> Learning and Rome alike in Empire grew;
> And Arts still followed where her Eagles flew;
> From the same foes, at last, both felt their doom,
> And the same age saw Learning fall, and Rome.
>
> . . . . .
>
> A second deluge Learning thus o'er-run,
> And the Monks finished what the Goths begun.[1]

Blake, on the other hand, completely reverses the verdict – and with equal conviction:

> Rome and Greece swept Art into their maw and destroyed it; a

[1] *An Essay on Criticism.*

warlike State can never produce Art. It will rob and plunder and accumulate into one place, and translate and copy and buy and sell and criticise, but not make. Grecian is Mathematic Form: Gothic is Living Form.[1]

And again:

The Classics! it is the Classics, and not Goths nor Monks, that desolate Europe with wars.[2]

Finally, a paradox from an historian. For almost two millennia the faith of Europe has been grounded on the Judaeo-Christian ethic. But read the sober *Annals* of the Roman historian, Tacitus, writing at the end of the first century of our era, and the language used to describe the adherents of both the Jewish and the Christian faiths is quite startling. He was genuinely appalled at the spread of Christianity to Rome which he described as 'the common sink into which everything infamous and abominable flows like a torrent from all quarters of the world'.[3]

Greek philosophers such as Zeno and Socrates delighted in teaching through contradiction. As we look back we see contradictions in their own lives and teaching. Often they were ambiguous or ambivalent or both. But in spite of this, and in spite of the fact that the writings of those prior to Plato have not survived they have left us a fascinating debate, hard hitting at times, and with the honours fairly evenly divided. Not at all typical was that young Greek who, on seeing his philosophy tutor stuck head foremost in a dyke, passed by and left someone of a less philosophic turn of mind to haul him out. When taxed with inhumanity the student replied that his tutor had impressed upon him that we could never have sufficient knowledge about any given matter to form a judgment; so, not knowing whether it was better or worse to rescue the man, he had left him in the dyke. The more typical Greek attitude was that scepticism was healthy, honest doubt a necessity, inaction in the face of contradictions useless.

SUGGESTED READING

Huxley, Aldous. *Literature & Science* (Chatto & Windus).

---

[1] *On Virgil* (Appendix to the Prophetic Books).
[2] Ibid.   [3] *Annals* XV.44 (Everyman's Library, Dent).

GP B

CHAPTER II

Roots in the Great Rivers

Measurement began our might;
Forms a stark Egyptian thought,

W. B. YEATS

All experience is an arch. . . .

TENNYSON

There was a story current in ancient Greece that one day the great god Zeus was smitten with a headache of cosmic proportions. His howling quickly brought other gods to the scene. Hermes, the worldly-wise, having some fore-knowledge of the cause, summoned Hephaestos the heavenly smith; he cleft open the head of Zeus, whereupon out leapt Pallas Athene, a goddess, fully grown, fully armed and full of wisdom; a goddess 'born without love and without biology'.

Much the same kind of birth used to be claimed for Greek philosophic thought which made its appearance in Europe and the seaboard of Asia Minor at the beginning of the sixth century before Christ and which was thought to be as lacking in ancestry as Athene. But this new rationalist movement did have antecedents and they are to be found, in the main, in the poems of Homer and Hesiod. Indeed it is doubtful if anyone today would be bold enough to draw a hard and fast line between the mythical events as recorded by the poets and the rationalised systems of the philosophers. The former may present profound scientific truths in mythological guise while the latter may have recourse to myth either because it enables them to present in graphic and familiar terms what they want to say or because their reason and knowledge have not advanced sufficiently far to dispel it.

Homer presents us with Zeus and his fractious family of gods already in possession of the refulgent plateau of Olympus. He is not concerned to record the earlier conflicts from which Zeus emerged victorious to rule this pantheon and to be hailed and worshipped as 'father of gods and of men'. Nor does he describe the primordial upheavals which produced our universe, the earlier generations of the immortals and the creatures of the earth. His immortals are almost unbelievably anthropomorphic, the celestial counterparts of a race of warlike, aristocratic chieftains and their ladies; they share in the whole gamut of human emotions and experiences – except for death. One example will be sufficient to enable us to catch the spirit of these Olympians as portrayed in *The Iliad*:

> Thus by the beaked ships the Achaeans drew up for battle round the indefatigable son of Peleus, and on the other side the Trojans too fell in, on the high ground of the plain. At the same time Zeus ordered Themis, from the summit of rugged Olympus, to call the gods to Assembly, and she went the rounds and summoned them to his Palace. . . .
>
> When all had foregathered in the Palace, the Earth-shaker Poseidon (who had not ignored the goddess's call, but had come up out of the sea to join them and had sat down in their midst) enquired what purpose Zeus might have in mind. 'Lord of the Lightning Flash,' he said, 'why have you ordered the gods to assemble? Are you concerned for the Trojans and Achaeans, who at this moment are about to come to grips once more?'
>
> 'Lord of the Earthquake,' replied Zeus the Cloud-compeller, 'you have read my mind aright and know why I have summoned this gathering. They do concern me even in their destruction. Nevertheless I propose to stay here and seat myself in some Olympian glen from which I can enjoy the spectacle. The rest of you have my permission to join the Trojans and Achaeans, and to give your help to either side as your sympathies dictate. . . .'
>
> These words from the son of Cronos unleashed the dogs of war. The immortals at once set out for the scene of action in two hostile groups. Hera and Pallas Athene made their way to the Achaean fleet. So did Poseidon the Girdler of the world, and Hermes the Bringer of Luck and the cleverest wonder-worker of them all. Hephaestus followed them, exulting in his enormous strength, for though he limped he was active enough on his slender legs. To the Trojan side went Ares in his flashing helmet, Phoebus of the Flowing Hair, Artemis, the Archeress, Leto, the River Xanthus, and laughter-loving Aphrodite.[1]

[1] *The Iliad*, Book XX, pp. 366-7 (Penguin).

From this single passage we may note the following points in Homer's view of his world and his gods:

1. Lightning, movements of clouds and earthquakes are not caused by natural forces but by Zeus and Poseidon.
2. Like a Homeric 'leader of men' Zeus exercises his prerogative of summoning the other gods, however powerful, to council but civilised discussion is permitted.
3. The gods, from Zeus downwards, are not only deeply concerned about the human race, they are passionately partisan. They side with both cities and heroes according to earlier compliments enjoyed or slights suffered.
4. A river is more than a river: it is a god.
5. Themis, the personification of law and order, and of justice in the world, is subject to the bidding of Zeus. We see that in spite of the unworthy and superior tone adopted by Zeus – 'I propose to stay here and seat myself in some Olympian glen from which I can enjoy the spectacle' – and in spite of the rather arbitrary and capricious atmosphere that prevails in Olympus, Themis is present, and that is of vital importance to man.

Hesiod, farmer and poet of Boeotia on the Greek mainland, was writing between the periods of the composition of the Iliad and the Odyssey and the appearance of the Ionian rationalists whom we shall be discussing in the next chapter. In his poem *The Theogony* he assembled, in an effort to account for the origin of the universe, the gods and man, mythological elements far more ancient and primeval than those which appear in Homer. It may be convenient to consider his poem firstly as a cosmogony, i.e. creation of the universe, and secondly as a theogony, i.e. the creation of the gods.

The essence of Hesiod's account is as follows. In the beginning all things consisted of one great mass fused together. The act which set creation in motion was the separating of the heaven and the earth:

> Verily at first Chaos came to be, but next wide-bosomed Earth, the ever-sure foundation of all the deathless ones who hold the peaks of snowy Olympus, and dim Tartarus in the depth of the wide-pathed Earth, and Eros (Love), fairest among the deathless gods, who unnerves the limbs and overcomes the mind and wise counsels of all gods and all men within them.[1]

[1] *The Theogony*, pp. 87-9 (Loeb Classical Library).

(It is important to note that here 'Chaos' means something specific: it is the 'yawning gap' between heaven and earth. Note, too, that Eros, Life Force and Principle of Attraction, is present from the start.)

Next came Night and Day and then:

> Earth first bare starry Heaven, equal to herself, to cover her on every side, and to be an ever-sure abiding place for the blessed gods. And she brought forth long hills, graceful haunts of the goddess-nymphs who dwell amongst the glens of the hills. She bare also fruitless deep with his raging swell, Pontus, without sweet union of love.[1]

However, now that the cosmos has been formed, Earth (Gaia) and Heaven (Ouranos) cease to be merely earth and heaven and become the primeval pair who produce the whole galaxy of Titans, monsters and gods with which the fertile imagination of the Greeks peopled the universe. The Titans born of Gaia and Ouranos included Cronos who, assisted by his mother, rebelled against his father and deposed him. Cronos is in turn deposed by his son, Zeus, who after a violent battle, first against the Titans, and then against the fire-breathing monster Typhoeus, emerges as victorious lord of the universe. He is the 'father of gods and of men' whom we have met in Homer and he apportions the spheres of interest in the way with which we are familiar in Greek religion: the heaven to himself, the sea to his brother Poseidon and the Lower World to another brother, Hades. Mount Olympus was to be shared in common. With the passing of power to the Olympians, the older gods do not cease to exist, but they become more shadowy and indistinct. It is interesting to note that the assistance and advice of Gaia is always available for each new generation in its moment of testing and struggle: in other words, as we might well expect, the power of mother earth is abiding.

Now the elements of Hesiod's *Theogony* have their origins in the mythologies of peoples of greater antiquity than the Greeks; particularly the peoples of the great river civilisations, Egypt and Babylonia. Historically there were points of contact between the Greeks and the civilisations of the near east which could well have accounted for the spread of such mythologies or it may have been that these were stored away in the folk-consciousness of the Greeks from the

[1] Ibid.

time they themselves migrated from the east (if indeed they did).
We find the following elements common to the mythologies of the
Egyptians, Babylonians, and Greeks as represented by Hesiod:

1. The separating of earth and sky. (There is a remarkable painting
   on an Egyptian coffin depicting the sky-goddess, Nut, forcibly
   separated by the god Shu, the Atlas of Egyptian mythology,
   and held in an arched position over her husband, Geb, the
   earth-god.)
2. The earth floats upon a waste of waters (and in Homer and
   Hesiod is surrounded by Okeanos). For obvious reasons, water
   has a greater predominance in the consciousness of the Egyptians
   and Babylonians.
3. All gods and life stem from one generating pair of gods.
4. There is violent hostility and struggle between father and son
   for successive generations until order is established.
5. The god youngest in time and representing the more advanced
   stage of civilisation fights and overcomes the more primitive
   forces; e.g. in the Babylonian epic, Marduk conquers Tiamat
   as, in Hesiod, Zeus conquers the Titans and the monster
   Typhoeus.

The physical environment has much to do with the forming not
only of the mythology but of the consciousness and culture of any
nation. This is particularly well illustrated in the cases of ancient
Babylonia and Egypt. Let us consider in greater detail how this
applies to the latter.

Life – in the most literal sense – and thought revolved about two
things: the diurnal habit of the sun and the annual habit of the river.
As the Greek traveller and historian Herodotus wrote:

> The Egypt to which we sail nowadays is, as it were, the gift of the
> river....[1]

This statement is fully brought home to us by the contemporary
scholar J. A. Wilson when he writes:

> The essential part of Egypt is a green gash of teeming life cutting
> across brown desert wastes. The line of demarcation between life
> and non-life is startlingly clear: one may stand at the edge of the
> cultivation with one foot on the irrigated black soil and one foot

[1] *The Histories*, p. 104 (Penguin).

on the desert sands. The country is essentially rainless; only the waters of the Nile make life possible where otherwise there would be endless wastes of sand and rock.[1]

As the body required food, so the producing of food was totally dependent on utilising the flood-waters of the Nile and the alluvial mud it carried down. This could be carried out adequately only if proper preparations had been made and the time of the inundation known in advance. This was the form Necessity took when she taught the Egyptian astronomer-priests before the year 4000 B.C. to calculate the length of a solar year as twelve months of thirty days each, plus five feast days. This prescience of the period of inundation was allied to a highly developed skill in the mathematics of surveying and the manipulating of water levels. The peasant population found it worth its while to support a class of priestly mathematicians without whom life would have been impossible.

The division of labour and the growth of a state machine was naturally accompanied by the calculation and collection of taxes. Taxes – paid in kind – required handbooks of the arithmetic of weights and measures and a facility in the mensuration of grain-growing land (geometry). It was quickly discovered that the easiest method of determining the size of irregular areas of alluvium-covered land was by dividing them into triangles with the result that the triangle, particularly when two of its sides contained an angle of 90°, assumed enormous importance in Egyptian life.

During the millennium which followed the calculation of the length of the solar year the Egyptians were gaining a facility in working with solid geometry in the form of baked brick. Just about one thousand years after the introduction of that calendar the Great Pyramid of Gizeh was constructed. For this the surveyors had to mark out an exact square on a plane which had been levelled with precision. They had to be sufficiently conversant with the practical manipulation of volumes to be able to construct the pyramid with blocks of stone, weighing between two and three tons, so accurately cut and dressed as to fit together leaving no crack between.

To accomplish such feats the surveyors and builders of the Pharaohs relied on plumb-line, set-square, inclined plane, river, sleds, organised man-power and, above all, the professional rope-knotters. Much depended on the skill and accuracy of these rope-knotters who

[1] *Before Philosophy*, pp. 39–40 (Pelican).

marked out right-angled triangles and squares. Imagine the treason-
able and sacrilegious chaos that would have been caused at the apex
of the pyramids at Gizeh if those men manipulating the rope had
been unreliable. The word 'hypotenuse' means simply the piece of
rope or cord stretched opposite the right angle. In day-to-day work
the Egyptians used as a ready-reckoner a type of abacus which consisted of grooves in the sand which could be filled with smooth
pebbles (the Latin for one of these pebbles was 'calculus'). There was
a groove for digits, tens, hundreds and thousands (so that 'carry one'
meant quite literally what it said). The base of ten had clearly come
down from the time of 'man the hunter' when the fingers were used
for reckoning. Twenty had been used as a base in early times – witness our word 'score' – but gradually gave way to the decimal scale
either because men found the latter more convenient or because the
supervisors of workmen began to cover up their toes.

Naturally in any consideration of ancient Egypt the question
arises: why pyramids? The answer to this leads us back from highly
sophisticated celestial and riparian geometry to primitive beliefs
about creation and cosmology.

The Egyptians believed that their land rested on the primeval
ocean which they called Nun. From the primal waters of Nun the
sun rose anew each morning and the Nile was renewed each year.
As early as there were men in Egypt to witness anything, they
noticed that, as the flood-waters of the Nile receded, any silt-covered
pinnacles and promontories of land were the first to burgeon into
life. It was not surprising therefore that they imagined the Creator
as coming forth from the waters and resting on a mound of earth.
The mound of earth rising from the waters beneath and touched by
the rays of the sun from above was synonymous with Life; the
pyramid is the mound in sacred, stylised form. The Pharaohs, at
rest in the heart of the massive symbol of the meeting place of silt
and sun, have eternal life assured.

One can see the compulsive force behind not only the enormous
monuments at Gizeh, but those significant guardians of Lake Moeris
which so impressed Herodotus. Of this lake he writes: '. . . the circumference of it is 3,600 stades, or sixty schoeni: a distance, that is
to say, of about 420 miles, equal to the length of the whole Egyptian
coastline; in shape it is elongated, running north and south, and its
greatest depth is fifty fathoms. Now this immense basin is obviously

artificial, for nearly in the middle of it are two pyramids, standing three hundred feet out of the water (with their bases an equal depth below the surface), and each surmounted by the stone image of a man sitting on a throne. The water in the lake is not supplied by natural springs (the country hereabouts being excessively dry), but has been brought from the Nile through an artificial duct, and flows in during six months of the year, and out again into the river during the other six.'[1]

The river produced more than pyramids and papyrus plants, corn and crocodiles; the very language grew out of it. Professor Wilson tells us that since the Egyptian took his orientation from the river, the source of life, the words for 'south' and 'face', and 'north' and 'back of the head' are the same or closely related; the word 'to go south' is the word 'to go upstream' and the word 'to go north' is the word 'to go downstream'. He only hints at the serious linguistic and psychological conflict which must have arisen for any traditionally-minded Egyptian merchant or ambassador who found himself on the river Euphrates going *south* and *downstream* at the same time.

'Measurement began our might'? It is a simple statement but charged with a certain underlying controversy. For the moment it is enough to note that in Egypt it was the acquired expertise in 'measurement' which created the prestige of the rope-knotters, the privilege of the priestly administrators, the permanence of the pyramids and the power – to say nothing of the immortality – of the Pharaohs.

The Egyptians measured – therein lay their strength – and philosophised little, if at all. The Greeks leapt boldly and brilliantly into the arena of speculative and, as far as possible, rational thought – there lay their strength – and measured too, but with limitations. For the most part, myth is accepted as part of a faith or it is rejected, according to the world outlook and temperament of those who hear it. The Ionian speculation which will be described in the following chapter was open to debate, to criticism, to improvement (or the opposite) in this or that detail.

[1] Op. cit., pp. 161-2.

SUGGESTED READING

Frankfort, H., Frankfort, Mrs H. A., Wilson, Jacobsen. *Before Philosophy* (Pelican).
Guthrie, W. K. C. *The Greeks and their Gods* (Methuen).
Herodotus. *The Histories* (Penguin).
Hesiod. *The Theogony* (Loeb Classical Library, Heinemann).
Homer. *The Iliad. The Odyssey* (Penguin).
Seltman, Charles. *The Twelve Olympians* (Pan).

CHAPTER III

The Ionians: Thales, Anaximander and Anaximenes

A question then, is education.

XENOPHON

It may be I should find Olympus vacant
If I should return. For I have heard a
    wonder:
Lands without gods; nothing but earth and
    water;

EDWIN MUIR: *Prometheus*

It was Homer and Hesiod chiefly who peopled Mount Olympus with its gods: it was the men from Miletus who first declared it vacant. Miletus was a thriving maritime city belonging to a section of the Greek race known as Ionians. These Ionians had settled along the heavily indented seaboard of Asia Minor. They were an active, adventurous-minded folk, engaged in lively commercial enterprise at home, daring military exploits abroad and the provision of transport for the world's goods from India to the Atlantic Ocean. They sailed with the Phoenicians, a globe-girdling race who imported to the Greeks novelties ranging from amber to an alphabet and who circumnavigated the continent of Africa. Their cities were bustling with an expanding economic life; bulging communities sent out swarming colonists to mark out new cities on the shores of Italy, France and the Black Sea; buildings were being erected on a new scale; engineers were boring their way through mountains to bring fresh water to wealthy palaces; sailors and ship-owners were working out new methods of navigation and compiling better almanacs; aristocrat and merchant clashed in bitter

struggles for supremacy and state control. Such communities produced, for the first time in Europe, men who had sufficient wealth,
sufficient leisure and sufficient independence of spirit to become the
fathers of European philosophy, men whose minds darted about the
universe as did their ships about the seas, whose minds stored up
simple observations on nature as their warehouses stored up goods.

Such was Thales of Miletus – numbered among the seven sages
of Greece – whom we know to have been active at the time of a
famous eclipse of the sun which astronomers tell us took place in
585 B.C. The questions which he and his contemporaries felt compelled to investigate were: Of what is this universe made? Can the
immense diversity of materials in the world be reduced to a common,
basic stuff? It was Thales' opinion that there was such a basic, unifying
stuff and that it was water. And although we may consider this
element altogether too insubstantial to be the primordial substance
of our 'preposterous pig of a world', a little consideration will show
why he arrived at such a conclusion.

Living as he did on the periphery of the great Persian empire,
Thales would have known the Babylonian creation myths and the
epic exploits of the god Marduk. We know that he travelled in
Egypt where he cleverly calculated by simple geometry the height
of the Great Pyramid. In Egypt he would have been influenced by
the priestly tradition of the birth of the land from the primeval
waters of Nun. He would have seen the pyramids of Lake Moeris
rising up from the surface of the water as a mighty memorial to the
truth of his thesis.

But our interest in these early thinkers is not so much for their
rationalisation of preceding mythologies as for the advances made
by common observation. Thales knew that without water men die;
that the vital processes of the human body require, if not water, a
fluid (indeed it is likely that the word which Thales used meant 'the
moist' rather than or as well as 'water'); that the very seed of life
and the embryo which it produces are dependent on a kind of water;
and he would certainly have noticed that when the watery element
had been squeezed out of the olive, the grape, the orange and the
peach, there was precious little left. (It was only a generation ago
that a Cambridge zoologist stated that even the Archbishop of
Canterbury was sixty-nine per cent water.)

The search for a basic substance has proceeded with increasing momentum since Thales first began it. It reached a climax in antiquity with the postulating of the atom. Early in the nineteenth century a certain William Prout put forward the claim that all was made of hydrogen. In this, the atomic century, it seemed as though the final answer to Thales' question might be something akin to electricity, but in spite of the unprecedented attack which has been mounted against the stronghold of the atom, the battle has yet to be won, the question has yet to be answered.

The mention of electricity brings us back to Thales in 600 B.C. Why, he wondered, did those knobs of Baltic amber when heated by friction attract other particles and sweep them up?

He could not have known the effect the action of rubbing had on the electrons of the amber, nor could he have foreseen the future significance of the word which was the Greek for amber – *elektron*.

The acquisitive society in which Thales lived was as prone as ours to measure a man's ability by his fortune. His friends taunted the philosopher with the uselessness of a life spent in seeking out first causes and the secrets of the universe – and the more so subsequent to a rumour that he had fallen into a well while gazing up at the stars. So Thales, according to the account found in Aristotle, having observed by signs of nature that the terraced olive groves around Miletus were going to yield a bumper harvest, quietly bought up all the available olive-presses. Now, olive oil was one of the most important commodities of the ancient world and when harvest time came round and it was discovered that 'the dreamer' held a corner in olive-presses, the unwary citizens of Miletus were forced to hire at exorbitant rates and Thales made a fortune.

.   .   .   .   .

Anaximander was a generation younger than Thales. He was not so expert an astronomer as his fellow citizen but in his efforts to account for the existence of the universe around him he combined imaginative and original thought with novel speculation to form a fascinating, if complicated, cosmogony.

In the beginning, said Anaximander, a stratified system made up of the four elements hung freely suspended in space. At the centre of the system was a core of earth, cylindrical in shape like the drum of a column. Encasing this core, rather in the way that bark encases the timber of a tree, were the other elements: first, water; then air (or mist); and finally an outermost stratum of fire. This enfolding fire naturally heated the mist and the water. As the water turned into mist, areas of dry land appeared. The mist increased in volume and burst through the encasing envelope of fire. This envelope, when distended to bursting-point, formed as it were wheels or hoops of fire which were then themselves enshrouded by outer covers of mist. The universe above us was permanently spanned by hoops of fire, but only where there was a hole in the surrounding tube of mist did the fire show through. These punctures in the opaque tubes of mist appeared to us as the stars and other heavenly bodies. The temporary sealing of these apertures accounted for eclipses.

And what of the Ionian question: 'Of what is the universe made?' Anaximander agreed with Thales that the myriad and apparently dissimilar substances of the universe might in reality be one and the same. But he held that this primal substance could not be water or, indeed, any one of the four elements mentioned. He argued that if any one of these elements were primary, it would, in time, devour the others and extend its empire at the cost of their existence. But this, he maintained, did not happen. He felt clearly that although opposing elements in this world encroached each on the other, some cosmic force maintained a balance, some kind of cosmic justice still prevailed. He saw on the Aegean shore that water encroached on land, but that under volcanic action the land reclaimed its own. He saw on the Anatolian uplands that the chill of night deposed the warmth of the day – but not for long. He saw surrounding empires expanding here, contracting there. And most keenly of all he would have been aware in his home city of the bitter ebb and flow of party strife now fiercer than in Thales' day. It is not coincidental but rather as the result of writing in a society which had many comparable features that Anaximander's feelings about the 'tug and scramble' of life and its opposing elements are so well summed up by Shakespeare when he wrote:

> Take but degree away, untune that string,
> And hark what discord follows! Each thing meets
> In mere oppugnancy. The bounded waters
> Should lift their bosoms higher than the shores
> And make a sop of all this solid globe.[1]

[1] *Troilus and Cressida*, Act I, Sc. 3.

So Anaximander, believing that all matter derived from some primordial substratum not yet identified, called it simply 'the stuff which has no limit'.

Thales had envisaged a flat earth floating on water, which forced upon him the difficulty of explaining what supported the water, and so on *ad infinitum*. Anaximander advanced at least to the point of making the earth cylindrical and cutting loose from that old problem of providing that infinite series of elephants, tortoises, and other cosmic props. He simply said that the earth, of necessity, remained in the middle of things, and left it at that. His boldness had brought him nearer to the truth.

But this was not Anaximander's only bold stroke. Having used his imagination to account for the earth in its physical context he then proceeded to account for the creatures which inhabited the earth. In so doing he formulated a theory, not a very thoroughgoing or comprehensive one, perhaps, but nevertheless a theory of evolution. This appears to have been based largely on the observation of the habits of fish in the Eastern Mediterranean. Anaximander was convinced that man could not have survived on the earth as the result of any sudden act of creation; for he thought that the extreme helplessness of infants, their slowness in learning to defend themselves and their long period of complete dependence on those who had already acquired a knowledge of nature precluded any such survival. Presumably he reasoned that the first adults would have been as lacking in experience and as easy a prey to predatory enemies as infants. He concluded that the most likely origin of man was the fish and that all other living creatures had emerged in some way from 'the moist element'.

When Anaximander expressed the view that living creatures originated in 'the moist element' he was giving expression to an equation which was not uncommon in the Middle East at that time: heat plus moist earth gives life. 'The moist element' was essential and seemed, as far as this enquiry went, to point back towards the primeval sea.

But whereas the Egyptians and Babylonians were accustomed to the perennial and prodigal sprouting of life from the alluvial mud, the Greeks were, in addition, inaugurating the study of marine biology. They were impressed by the habits of certain types of viviparous sharks and dog-fish which they must have observed closely.

There was one type of dog-fish which appeared to allow its young to issue forth at feeding time and appeared to gather them back into the protecting body on the approach of danger. This was possibly the kind of protective act which to Anaximander was the pre-requisite if a species were to survive, let alone evolve. We do know that Aristotle made a detailed anatomical study of the dog-fish as part of his comprehensive biological survey and the fact that evidence of earlier studies has not survived does not mean that they were never undertaken. So we cannot rule out the possibility that the ana-tomical similarities between man and fish, now familiar to any student of biology, were also known to these Ionian thinkers. At any rate it was they who quietly set off a train of thought which rocked the world with full explosive force with the publication of Darwin's work one hundred years ago.

. . . . .

The third member of this Milesian group, Anaximenes, continuing the speculative quest for the underlying substance, concluded that it did indeed exist, and that it was one of the four elements already discussed: it was, in his opinion, air.

Although we have no writings extant, we know the kind of every-day experience which led Anaximenes to his conclusion. He knew that water was turned into vapour every time a copper-full was boiled, and that vapour turned into water every time it rained. He knew that when water turned to ice, a volatile liquid had become an unyielding solid. In the busy factories of the port he knew that all day long and every day, by subjection to pressure, soft wool became more solid felt; that in every blast furnace the air forced out under pressure through the bellows' nozzle increased the burning flame, while the action of the flame upon the solid ore produced a molten stream.

The elements, in fact, seemed interchangeable, appearing differ-ently at different times according to the degree of rarefaction or con-densation to which each was subjected. Fire was rarefied air; water was air condensed; and solid earth was but the form assumed by water when pressurised on a cosmic scale. A point was always reached where an increase in the amount of rarefaction or condensa-tion of matter resulted in a change of form.

Anaximenes' way of thinking has a curiously modern tang. We do know that the distinguishing feature of a gas, a liquid or a solid is the degree of mobility allowed the molecules in relation to their neighbours, and that a change in pressure, particularly when allied with a change in temperature, can bring about the very changes Anaximenes had in mind. It is perfectly true that the elements of which this world is composed did once exist in a gaseous state; and it is perfectly true that in the course of this world's evolution, those elements, subject to changing pressure and temperature, 'separated out' – to use the Ionians' phrase – into the forms we find them in today. From the complexities of interstellar rocketry to the simplicity of household heating we are now familiar with liquid gases and gaseous liquids.

Having then established mutability of the elements, Anaximenes assigned to air not only primacy over the others but the role of vital principle. 'As our soul', he wrote, 'being air, holds us together, so do breath and air surround the whole universe.' What soul does for man, air does for the universe: it gives it being. Here, a glance at some familiar words may help to bring out Anaximenes' meaning more clearly. The Greek word *psyche* meant breath before it meant soul, as did the Latin words *anima* and *spiritus*. The author of Genesis used similar language and a similar idea when he wrote: 'And the Lord God (i.e. a spirit) formed man of the dust of the ground and breathed into his nostrils the breath (i.e. psyche) of life and man became a living (i.e. animate) soul.' As Anaximenes would have said: 'Psyche, anima or air held together the dust that was man.'

A word of explanation is necessary here when talking of air in Greek philosophy. The Greeks used two words: *aither*, by which they indicated the upper reaches of the atmosphere – say, from about the top of Mount Olympus upwards and *aer*, the impure mixture of mist, vapour and air which swirls about us earth-bound mortals. The former is almost invariably closely associated with purified fire and divinity. It is not uncommon, therefore, for the four elements to appear as: earth, mist, fire and water.

Such then were the systems of these early Ionian thinkers. However inadequate or naive they may appear now to us, they marked a new and bold departure in the thinking of their day. They attempted to provide a purely rational account of the phenomena of the universe, relying not upon the arbitrary acts of anthropomorphic

deities but upon such of nature's laws as they could formulate. Their
strength was an almost childlike confidence in the evidence of the
senses; their method was to project on to the wide screen of the
universe what they saw and knew of nature in their daily lives.
Anaximenes, seeing the leaf held aloft in upward currents of air,
assumed that the broad disc of the earth could be similarly suspended;
and seeing the transformations of earth's ore effected on a limited
scale at the bellows' mouth, assumed that similar transformations
had been effected throughout the universe since time began.

To these Ionians, anxious as they were to prise out nature's secrets
and to understand the world in which they lived, the old anthropomorphic gods of Homer and the Egyptian priests were nothing but
outmoded and inhibiting impediments to progress. Compared with
the Egyptian in his well defined and extremely rigid social structure,
the Greek of the Ionian maritime communities enjoyed incomparable freedom of physical and intellectual movement; and so it
was that some fifteen years after Anaximenes was in his prime, an
Ionian poet, Xenophanes, was able to write:

> But if oxen (and horses) and lions had hands or could draw with
> hands and create works of art like those made by men, horses
> would draw pictures of gods like horses, and oxen of gods like
> oxen, and they would make the bodies (of their gods) in accord-
> ance with the form that each species itself possesses.[1]

SUGGESTED READING

(For this and subsequent chapters)

Armstrong, A. H. *An Introduction to Ancient Philosophy* (Methuen).
Burnet, J. *Greek Philosophy* (Thales to Plato) (Macmillan).
Farrington, B. *Greek Science* (Pelican).
Guthrie, W. K. C. *In the Beginning: Some Greek views on the origins of life and
    the early state of man* (Methuen).
Sambursky, S. *The Physical World of the Greeks* (Routledge).

---

[1] *Ancilla to the Pre-Socratic Philosophers* (Diels, *Fragmente der Vorsokratiker*,
trs. Kathleen Freeman), p. 22, Fr. 15 (Blackwell).

CHAPTER IV

Pythagoras: Mathematics and Mysticism

I have sought for a joy without pain,
For a solid without fluctuation.

WILLIAM BLAKE

Mathematician, mystic, philosopher, physicist and politician, Pythagoras by his extraordinary versatility built up a number of reputations and has deeply influenced the whole stream of human thought.

He came from the island of Samos, which produced in the ancient world an outstanding crop of explorers, engineers, astronomers and mathematicians. Pythagoras, after extensive travel in Egypt and Babylonia, on returning to his native Samos, found the rule of the tyrant Polycrates increasingly distasteful; so he emigrated and founded a religious community in Croton in southern Italy. Not only did he and the members of his brotherhood engage in the serious pursuit of wisdom and knowledge, they also advocated salvation through holiness and a distinctive way of life. In this they differed from their predecessors of Miletus who were not in any sense concerned with advocating a way of life.

To some extent Pythagoras had much in common with Thales. He had listened to the priests of Egypt and Babylonia, and he was an outstanding geometer and mathematician. Further, when he set out to create his system of philosophy, he did so, as did the Milesians, in terms of workaday objects which he knew. But he went much further; for not only did he observe, he initiated controlled experiment and tested his results. And the basis of his work and observation? Precious stones, cut and set for merchant and aristocrat, and the seven-stringed well-tuned lyre.

Pythagoras had been apprenticed to his father who was an engraver of gems. In this highly skilled and meticulous work he became familiar with those crystalline shapes with which his mathematical and mystical imagination constructed the solid bodies of the universe. For example, from Pythagoras to Kepler the cube came to represent the earth and the dodecahedron the heavens. As Dr Seltman wrote in his brilliant essay on Pythagoras in *Riot in Ephesus*: 'Quartz crystal would give him a perfect pyramid; iron pyrites is found in cubes massed together; the dodecahedron is found in nature in the common garnet; and the beryl is a cylindrical hexagon.'[1]

We must guard against thinking that Pythagoras considered that the earth was a cube in shape or that the heavens consisted of a twelve-sided solid. No! These crystalline shapes were merely symbols which mystically represented the heavenly bodies and these shapes have figured large in the history of the occult ever since. In point of fact Pythagoras believed the earth to be a sphere – and he was the first to do so – not as the result of scientific calculation, but because the sphere was the perfect shape. And here, the word 'perfect' has not only a geometric but a moral connotation.

Crystallography, however, provided but the first step in the building of a cosmology by Pythagoras. Although his crystal solids from ephemeral ice (*krustallos* in Greek meant 'ice' before it meant 'rock-crystal') to unchanging diamond were substances well nigh stable enough with which to construct a universe, the mathematician in the man knew of something more changeless still. It is a commonplace that the more unstable and insecure is his world, the more eager is man's search for that which is stable, enduring and immune from the inexorable reversals of fortune. Pythagoras had returned from the Persian Empire where the Great King was a despot, where life was cheap and man's fortune subject to brutal sudden reversal. He had fled from his native Samos where the unlucky tyrant Polycrates was tempting fortune in his own peculiar way. And in his adoptive city, Croton, political feeling ran so high that, according to tradition, Pythagoras lost both his house and his life before the fury of a frenzied mob. So it is not surprising that the idea at the heart of his system was something which was for him the one eternal and unchanging concept; and that was Number.

[1] *Riot in Ephesus* (Max Parrish).

But back to the crystals! One aspect of these geometrical solids which fascinated Pythagoras and subsequent mathematicians such as Plato, was the relationship between the faces, vertices and edges. For example the cube must have eight vertices, twelve edges and six faces which will be square; the twenty-sided figure must have twelve vertices, thirty edges and twenty faces which will all be triangular. Not unnaturally, in working on these relationships Pythagoras denoted a point, or vertex, by one or one dot; he denoted a line, or edge, by two dots; a triangle by three; and a square by four, thus:

So he spoke of triangular numbers and square numbers. Then he thought of these plane surfaces as adding up to form solids. In this way, by thinking of number as representing spatial and physical entities, he could build up a world on a basis of number. Because one dot, two dots, three dots and four dots added up to ten, this number assumed magic qualities and the figure ten became the sacred symbol of the Pythagorean Brotherhood.

A certain primitive idea which was fundamental to Pythagoras' philosophy was that number could be identified and endowed with both moral and biological qualities. The number one was identified with Reason: it was not just an ordinary number; it was the fount and origin, the primal atom, as it were, from which all other number was derived. Two stood for opinion and four for justice. Further, apart from one, the odd numbers were male, the even numbers female. The union of the primary female number, two, with the primary male number, three, gave the figure five which was the perfect marriage number.

To us it may seem grotesque to assign gender and human characteristics to number, but it may assist us to recall that the irrational

lure of astrology, coming from Babylonia, pervaded the ancient
world just as it does certain areas of our life today. We may recall
too that in astrology each section of the Zodiac is associated with a
precious stone and each precious stone is endowed with a human
characteristic. This was so in the time of Pythagoras. For example,
the word 'amethyst' means in Greek, 'the one who can hold his
drink', 'diamond' means 'the unconquerable'.

If then for Pythagoras the basic form, the ultimate truth of the
component parts of the universe, was Number, his next logical step
was to investigate by what laws the component parts were joined
together to make a coherent, working whole. How was universal
equilibrium maintained – in so far as it was maintained? Anaximander, the Milesian, had said there was a kind of cosmic justice
which regulated the 'encroaching' of one element upon the territory
of another. Pythagoras set about uncovering these laws in a more
thoroughgoing manner than any of his predecessors. It is recorded,
too, that he was the first to assign the name 'kosmos' to the universe
which he was investigating. The word 'kosmo-logos' simply means
the science of order. It arose when man first looked at the movement
of the universe in which he found himself and asked whether it
worked at random or according to established laws which could be
investigated and formulated. ('Cosmetics' has to do with decorating
in accordance with 'the order and harmony' of line and colour.)

In seeking to reveal this 'order and harmony' Pythagoras turned
to a branch of science which easily admitted of investigation, and in
so doing, he provided one of the rare examples of controlled experiment in the pre-Socratic world. The branch of science was acoustics.
The apparatus required was simple enough: reed pipes of different
lengths; wine jars, identical in shape but containing varying volumes
of liquid; foundry hammers of different weights; and vibrating
strings which could be tightened or relaxed. The outcome of such
experiment was that not only did Pythagoras discover that the pitch
of a note depended on the frequency of the vibrations – the higher
pitch being produced by the more rapidly vibrating string – but that
the four fixed strings of the Greek lyre produced their familiar harmony by being in the ratio 6:8:9:12. The two extremes 6 and 12
gave the octave; 9 was the arithmetic mean and 8 the harmonic
mean of 6 and 12. The notes in music could, therefore, be represented
by numbers; and the harmonies, the laws which governed their

working relationships, could be represented as numerical ratios. Here was an extension of the idea that shapes and solids were numbers. Indeed the concepts of number-harmony and number-shape were combined when Pythagoras pointed out that the numbers of the cube were in the ratio 6 (faces): 8 (apexes): 12 (edges). The answer now to the question 'What is the basic stuff of the universe?' is Number, assembled according to certain laws of ratio and harmony. And harmony has been found to be a mean between two extremes – an idea which ran like a thread through Greek thought from that time onwards.

We have seen that the method of the Milesians had been to project on to the whole universe such laws as they found valid for more homely and accessible areas of it. This is precisely what Pythagoras did in forming his cosmology. The earth, he said, was spherical and revolved round a great central fire. We never see this fire because we are on that part of the earth which is turned away from it – just as a person on the far side of the moon would never see the earth.

Around this central fire revolved also the sun, the moon, the five planets and the great dome-like canopy in which were set the fixed stars. That made a total of nine spheres encircling the central universal hearth, and to complete the holy Decad, Pythagoras postulated a counter-earth (an idea he may well have imported from the Egyptian priests who liked to have their universe symmetrical). Harking back to his findings in acoustics he concluded that each sphere as it rode through space produced its own note. The pitch of the note depended on the speed of the revolution – those bodies which were further from the centre moving at greater speed and so giving forth a higher note. These notes, then, varying according to the distance of each body from the centre made up a cosmic harmony. Planetary motion was music and was known thenceforth as The Music of the Spheres. God, Number, Harmony was in the heavens and all was well with the confraternity of Croton – until . . .

Until one day the men who believed that 'everything that can be known has a Number' discovered that a hitherto simple, finite line, consisted of an infinite number of points which could not be known. The men who believed that Number was rational, discovered numbers which were irrational. The men who believed that between the hypotenuse and the sides of a right-angled triangle there existed a relationship which was harmonious and beautiful found that if the hypotenuse were the diagonal of a square, it was incommensurable with the side of that square. Here was a string which could not be tuned, a discord which could not be resolved. If we can imagine a good abbot assembling the brothers of his community and announcing to them that their theology was without foundation, we can perhaps imagine the shock with which the Pythagoreans had to accept the discovery that irrational Number not only could but did exist. This was no mere mathematical discovery for them; it was an event which knocked the bottom out of their universe, an event which robbed them of their certainty. Not very surprisingly, perhaps, it appears that they attempted to suppress the news of the discovery and, according to tradition, they believed that one of their number who met his end by drowning at sea had only received his fitting retribution for having divulged the secret without permission.

In all this, there was a certain cruel irony for the Pythagoreans and a salutary lesson for subsequent closed communities. The irony was that it had been one of Pythagoras' great achievements to prove the theorem associated with his name. The Egyptians and Babylonians knew that triangles with, for example, sides of ratio 3:4:5 or 5:12:13 contained a right angle and used the knowledge in their daily building and measuring. But it was Pythagoras – and here we have a typical example of the difference between Egyptian and Greek methods – who introduced the idea of proof and universal truth. When he proved that in a right-angled triangle the square on the hypotenuse equals the sum of the squares on the other two sides Pythagoras felt that he had been privileged to catch a glimpse of the eternal; the gem-cutter had unearthed a small kernel of truth more enduring than diamond and valid not only in the lapidary's workshop or the philosopher's school, but anywhere in the universe. Tradition holds that on completion of the proof, Pythagoras in great excitement performed an immensely costly sacrifice to the God who, as Plato later wrote, 'is always geometrising'.

The salutary lesson lies in the folly of those who search for truth suppressing it when it comes. The discovery of irrational numbers was not, in fact, the seismic disaster the Pythagorean took it to be. It was rather a stepping-stone on the path leading to a further branch of mathematics – approximations. To quote Professor Sambursky:

The method of approximations replaced the lost Pythagorean harmony and so became a powerful tool for the comprehension of both mathematical and physical realities. Here science learned the great lesson that this reality can only be approached gradually by innumerable approximations.[1]

The lesson was pointed poetically by Blake when he cried bitterly:

> I have sought for a joy without pain,
> For a solid without fluctuation.[2]

SUGGESTED READING

Heath, T. L. *A History of Greek Mathematics* (Oxford).
Heath, T. L. *A Manual of Greek Mathematics* (Oxford).

[1] *The Physical World of the Greeks*, pp. 34-5 (Routledge).
[2] *The Book of Urizen*, Ch. II, ll. 54-5.

CHAPTER V

Pythagoras and Orpheus

World-famous golden-thighed Pythagoras
Fingered upon a fiddle-stick or strings
What a star sang and careless Muses heard.

W. B. YEATS

Stop beating the dog; for I recognise in its
cry the soul of a departed friend of mine.

Attributed to PYTHAGORAS

It is typical of Pythagoras to turn up in a second chapter. But
there is a weighty legacy of his to be considered before we can
get to grips with 'that enquiring man', Heracleitus.
When Shakespeare wrote:

Most sacrilegious murder hath broke ope
The Lord's anointed temple, and stole thence
The life o' the building.

Macbeth, Act II, Sc. 1

and

Look how the floor of heaven
Is thick inlaid with patines of bright gold;
There's not the smallest orb which thou beholdest
But in his motion like an angel sings,
Still quiring to the young-eyed cherubims:
Such harmony is in immortal souls;
But, whilst this muddy vesture of decay
Doth grossly close it in, we cannot hear it.

Merchant of Venice, Act V, Sc. 1

he was giving expression to an idea which Pythagoras first incorporated into Greek philosophy. Pythagoras took the idea from a
religious sect associated with the legendary figure of Orpheus and

transmitted it to Plato who fixed it firmly as the base of so much in European literature and thought. So marked was the affinity between the Orphics and Pythagoreans that, although several centuries separated the two founders, the writings of the two sects were frequently confused.

Put most briefly, the important facts in the Orphic system were these. The young god, Dionysus, son of Zeus, was torn asunder and devoured by the Titans. For this sin of devouring that which was divine, Zeus blasted the Titans, and from their ashes, still impregnated with the blood of the slain god, man was formed. Dionysus was recreated and became the central figure of Orphic worship and ritual.

Here we have, stated in religious and symbolic terms, the great dualism which enters Greek philosophy at this point and which persists as one of the central problems through all philosophy. Is there such a thing as soul capable of independent and perpetual existence, and if there is, what is its relationship to the body? Linked with this goes an attendant problem with dual aspect. If we live in a divinely appointed universe, how are we to account for the parallel existence of good and evil, particularly when, as so often is the case, evil appears to predominate?

Orphic doctrine taught that man, compounded as he was from Titan and godhead, was part sinful, part divine. Soul, the immortal part, suffered this attachment to the body, 'this muddy vesture of decay', as punishment for original sin, viz. the killing and eating of Dionysus. The Greek word for 'body' was *soma*; one of their words for 'tomb' was *sema*; so with their typical love of playing upon words, the Greeks were for ever cogitating on this two-headed problem – the 'soma-sema' relationship. As one Pythagorean writer put it: '... because of certain punishments the soul is yoked to the body and buried in it as in a tomb'. The followers of Orpheus were keenly aware that man had been created with a nature divided against itself; were keenly aware of the paradox that by appetite came life and the perpetuation of the race and that also by appetite came downfall and death.

How then did the adherents of this religion attain salvation and escape that contradiction by which nature was bedevilled? By mortification of the body and constant cherishing of the soul they endeavoured to maintain the two as separate as possible so that in the end and at the day of dissolution the soul might run free. By initiation into the Orphic mysteries – based probably on the descent of Orpheus to the underworld – participants were afforded some slight foreknowledge of life after death and some acquaintance with the labyrinthine intricacies of Hades through which the soul must later pass. And finally, by repeating the sin for which the soul was making atonement, i.e. by consuming their god, Dionysus, ritually in the form of wine, they enabled the soul to practise a limited and temporary form of ecstasy – taking ecstasy in its precise meaning of 'standing out or apart from' the body. The whole exercise is rather reminiscent of the prisoner being released from the dungeon for a little exercise so that chafed limbs retain something of their former power and so that dimmed eyes be gently accustomed to the light of the sun.

The belief which is most popularly associated with Pythagoras and which holds a prominent place in Plato's scheme of things is that of the transmigration of souls. This, too, was an important section of the Orphic creed. It was part of a carefully inculcated system of punishment and reward to which the soul would be subjected after the dissolution of the body. There was a scale – albeit a rather haphazard one – of promotion and demotion for souls according to whether they had eschewed or embraced the pleasures of the flesh while on earth. More important still, the soul of the truly devout Orphic could find release from 'the wheel of birth' and be granted eternal peace after fewer reincarnations than the uninitiated.

In the closing pages of his celebrated *Republic* Plato tells the tale of a soldier called Er who, ten days after meeting death in battle, came to life on his very funeral pyre. Not of least interest among the extraordinary tableaux witnessed by Er in the world below was the exchanging of souls by the famous dead. Agamemnon, for example, hateful of mankind as a result of much suffering, took on the life of an eagle. Atalanta, renowned in life for athletic prowess, was unable to resist selecting the life of an athlete because of the honours which would accrue. Epeius, the carpenter who constructed the fateful wooden horse at Troy, was converted to the form of a craftswoman. The soul of poor, malformed, chattering Thersites found itself clothed by an ape. And finally, the soul of Odysseus, sated with deeds of fame and endurance, went around ferreting out 'a life of quiet obscurity'.

Not only did the Pythagoreans adopt and teach the theory of metempsychosis: they also proved it to be true. 'For', they said, 'did the master not on a certain occasion at Olympia allow the spectators to catch a glimpse of his golden thigh, showing that he was indeed the reincarnation of Midas of the golden touch?'

So it came about that Pythagoras the engraver of gems, astronomer, physicist and mathematician found himself leader of a mystic brotherhood. Not only did he solemnly hold that the earth was a sphere and was not the centre of its system; not only did he conduct the earliest controlled experiments in acoustics; not only did he search out truth through the medium of mathematics; he also displayed what Plato referred to as 'a holy and quite distinctive way of life'. To an interesting degree he mingled in his own person the empiric nature of the Ionians from Miletus with the mysticism of the Orphics.

From this point onwards in the history of thought have run two widely divergent streams. The one is made up of those who believe that knowledge is to be apprehended by way of experience, trial and error and who call themselves empiricists (from the Greek verb *empeirasthai*: to make trial of). To the other adhere those – the *a-priorists* – who claim that truth is approached by purely mental processes based on given principles and that contemplation is the highest form of activity.

When Pythagoras, as a result of purely mental activity, peeped beyond the veil and was granted his moment of truth, he might well, like Simeon, have lifted up his voice and chanted: 'Lord, now lettest thou thy servant depart in peace according to thy word. For mine eyes have seen thy salvation. . . .'[1] For that is precisely what 'theorem' means – something which has been seen.

SUGGESTED READING

Guthrie, W. K. C. *Orpheus and Greek Religion* (Methuen).

[1] *St. Luke's Gospel*, Ch. 2, vv. 29-30.

CHAPTER VI

Heracleitus of Ephesus

Without contraries there is no progression.
For he saw that Life lived upon Death:
The Ox in the slaughter-house moans.

WILLIAM BLAKE

All things are in a state of flux.

HERACLEITUS

One day in the first quarter of the fifth century B.C. a curious, haughty old man came down from the mountains into the city of Ephesus. He was known variously as the Dark Man or the Riddler, and since he had found both the common people and the rulers of his city of Ephesus equally intolerable he had betaken himself to the surrounding mountains, there to live as a misanthropic hermit with no more than grass for his precarious sustenance. And now he had come back with disease in his body and a riddle on his lips. The riddle was for the doctors; but whether it was because they did not understand it, or because they knew no cure for the ailment, or because the patient was accustomed to speak scathingly of their profession, nothing was done. So Heracleitus, with a spirit of independence which was typical, prescribing his own treatment, went off and buried himself up to the neck in dung from the midden-heap adjacent to the cowstall.

The riddle which Heracleitus had put to the doctors was: could they make a drought out of rainy weather? The disease he was suffering from was dropsy. The treatment was a simple and logical attempt to steam off the excess liquid from the body by surrounding it with the steaming dung. The experiment did not achieve the success its courageous simplicity deserved, and Heracleitus died.

This is a somewhat simplified account of a tradition which contains many uncertainties. However, that these precise events did or did not take place in this exact sequence is not here the important point. What is of importance for the full understanding of Greek thought of this period is to note what is implied in Heracleitus' action. Firstly, it indicates a willingness to rely on the validity of everyday observation. Secondly, it illustrates nicely the speculative method and the aptitude for inductive reasoning of the Ionians (i.e. reasoning from the particular to the general). Heracleitus, familiar with the particular instance of a pot boiling dry or a roof drying off after rain, boldly reasoned that the giving off of any steam would cause the drying up of any liquid associated with it. Thirdly, the unpleasant nature of the remedy was no deterrent (we are reminded that the Hippocratic doctors in the best Ionian tradition, in order to extend their knowledge and heal their patients, were prepared to examine the human faeces with four of the five senses).

Before he died, Heracleitus had written one book which he deposited as an offering in the great temple of Diana at Ephesus. It was his encyclopaedic contribution to existing world knowledge, covering as it did, metaphysics, politics and science. This book was written in an oracular style – not an uncommon one in authors as highly aristocratic as Heracleitus – and although the book itself has not survived, over one hundred of these oracular sayings have been preserved. Without these, Greek philosophical writing, and perhaps it is no exaggeration to say all philosophical writing, would be very much the poorer.

Heracleitus took up the great question where Thales, Anaximander and Anaximenes, the Milesians over the border in West Caria, had left it about half a century before. Firstly, water, then an indeterminate, infinite 'something', and then air had been put forward as the basic stuff from which the whole universe was ultimately derived. The Ephesian aligned himself with the Milesian in his conviction that all was reducible to a single substance. What was the substance and what the cycle of its transformations?

> This ordered universe (cosmos), which is the same for all, was not created by any one of the gods or of mankind, but it was ever and is and shall ever be ever-living Fire, kindled in measure and quenched in measure.[1]

Or again, in the form of a simile: 'There is an exchange: all

[1] *Ancilla to the Pre-Socratic Philosophers*, p. 26, Fr. 30.

things for Fire and Fire for all things, like goods for gold and gold for goods.'[1]

And the cycle? 'The changes of fire: first, sea; and of sea, half is earth and half fiery waterspout. . . . Earth is liquefied into sea, and retains its measure according to the same Law as existed before it became earth.'[2] And again, perhaps more clearly: 'Fire lives the death of earth, and air lives the death of fire; water lives the death of air, earth that of water.'[3] So with Fire as the primary material from which all originates and to which all eventually returns, the basic scheme is:

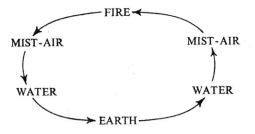

Convinced of the truth of this cosmic cycle, Heracleitus concluded that: 'The way up and down is one and the same.'[4]

As he went about the squares of Ephesus, the busy seaboard towns of Ionia and the inland mountains, trying to unravel for himself the realities of the universe, Heracleitus became convinced that there was another great constant: paradoxically enough, this was CHANGE. This principle of change is the one most commonly associated with him. 'Everything is in a state of flux', he said, 'and nothing abides. In the same river, we both step and do not step, we are and we are not. It is impossible to touch the same mortal substance twice, but through the rapidity of change. . . .'[5]

This change does not, of course, proceed equally obviously or at an equal rate in all things. Although the ring is eventually worn thin by the finger and the paving stone is worn hollow by the passing of bare feet, the process is unobtrusive and slow and not at all like the violent exchange when sea is translated to fire (or air) through the

[1] Ibid., p. 31, Fr. 90.
[2] Ibid., p. 27, Fr. 31.
[3] Ibid., p. 30, Fr. 76.   [4] Ibid., p. 29, Fr. 60.
[5] Ibid., p. 31, Fr. 91.

dread waterspout or when a man of some importance in his own city becomes a slave through war. Often, too, we are heedless of the change as was the old woodman who avowed he had had the same faithful axe for forty years though it had had two new heads and three new handles.

Whether the movement of things coming into being and passing away was gentle or violent, gradual or instantaneous, apparent or concealed, it was, thought Heracleitus, controlled by universal Law. It appeared to him, as it had to Anaximander, that some kind of cosmic justice was at work which saw to it that the elements did not overstep their allotted bounds in time or space, that the 'ever-living Fire' was 'kindled in measure and quenched in measure'. This concept of 'measure' which runs like a thread through Greek thought is constantly stressed both in private life and in nature. He says 'Moderation is the greatest virtue...'[1] and, 'The sun will not transgress his measures; otherwise the Furies, ministers of Justice, will find him out.'[2]

The whole range of religious Mysteries and in particular the Orphic worship of Dionysus with all its totemistic rites and taboos disgusted Heracleitus. He wrote that the activities and revels of these 'night-ramblers, magicians, Bacchants, Maenads and Mystics' were unholy and shameless. Nor did Pythagoras himself escape these strictures: 'Much learning does not teach one to have intelligence; for it would have taught Hesiod and Pythagoras....'[3] This was not merely the natural antagonism between aristocrat and proletarian escapist religion – it is almost certain that Orphism and the under-privileged were closely linked – but rather the antagonism of one who was confident that the world was capable of rational explanation and that it would be a much more congenial place if man would try to understand natural philosophy.

But there was also a specific point of philosophy where Heracleitus was at variance with Pythagoras; a point which was central to his whole thought. Pythagoras when wrestling with the problem of good and evil, body and soul, had resorted to a mythological dualism. His disciples were accustomed to meditate on the mystery of pairs of opposites such as:

---

[1] Ibid., p. 32, Fr. 112.
[2] Ibid., p. 31, Fr. 94.
[3] Ibid., p. 27, Fr. 40.

STRAIGHT and CURVED
ONE and PLURALITY
ODD and EVEN
REST and MOVEMENT
LIMITED and UNLIMITED
MALE and FEMALE

and they concluded that the best life consisted in the discovery of a harmony which was a mean of two extremes.

Heracleitus too was fascinated by similar pairs of opposites; he too felt impelled to account for the existence of good and evil, life and death, war and peace. Rejecting a dualistic approach, he formulated the idea that any pair of opposites formed a unity; that the tension between warring contraries is, as it were, the mainspring of the universe; and that wisdom is the understanding of this unity. He wrote: 'That which is in opposition is in concert, and from things that differ comes the most beautiful harmony. One should know that war is general and jurisdiction is strife, and everything comes about by way of strife and necessity. Homer was wrong in saying, "Would that strife might perish from amongst gods and men." For if that were to occur, then all things would cease to exist.'[1]

From the imagery used we can see some of the simple, everyday objects which influenced his thought. For example: 'They do not understand how that which differs with itself is in agreement: harmony consists of opposing tension, like that of the bow and the lyre.'[2] Heracleitus, partly no doubt through his admiration for the great oracular centres of the ancient world which relied on their adroitness to coin the right *double entendre* in their responses, and partly because of his fascination for opposites, was intrigued by his own punning statement: 'The bow is called Life, but its work is death.'[3] (The Greek word *bios* means 'bow' and 'life'; only the accent differs.)

Heracleitus' answer, therefore, to such questions as: 'Why evil? Why war?' would be something like this:

[1] Ibid., pp. 25, 30, Fr. 8, 80.
[2] Ibid., p. 28, Fr. 51.
[3] Ibid., p. 28, Fr. 48.

WITHOUT EVIL – NO GOOD
WITHOUT DEATH – NO LIFE
WITHOUT WAR – NO PEACE
WITHOUT BODY – NO SOUL
WITHOUT MATTER – NO MIND.

(As a contemporary poet has written:

'So eyes must weep lest eyes should cease to shine.') And again, it is meaningless to ask 'Which is the more important side of the coin, the reverse or the obverse?' Or, 'Which is the more valuable extreme of the musical scale and which the more harmonious mean?' Clearly both coin and scale must be considered as a unit.

Since we live in the atomic age we may feel compelled to consider more closely Heracleitus' statements concerning war and strife. When he says: 'War is both king of all and father of all . . .' and, 'One should know that war is general and jurisdiction is strife . . .' does he mean 'war' in its specific, accepted sense, or does he mean the word to be synonymous with tension and strife generally? For, after all, he has said that without tension the universe would collapse. Yet in a statement attributed to Heracleitus, he says: 'War and Zeus are the same.' And the word used is *polemos*, war. Quite apart from this, commentators have been much exercised to know whether Heracleitus believed that at the end of a given cycle the whole world might revert to flame in a cosmic conflagration. It is, however, fairly certain that this idea had no place in his system. For Plato pointed out that Heracleitus, with perfect consistency, said that the One was always many, and the Many always one. Besides, the concept of the grand conflagration would run directly counter to the stated principle that 'ever-living Fire was kindled *in measure* and quenched *in measure*'. The whole concept of *ekpurosis* or 'finale by fire' was later grafted on to the Heracleitean cosmology by the pyrotechnical pontifications of the Stoics and certain sects of Christians – or was until the advent of nuclear fission.

These linked concepts of a constant cycle of change and the unity of opposites have been seminal in European thought from the sixth century B.C. to the present day. They form the basis of the dialectic movement which Socrates and Plato elevated, which Hegel and Marx placed at the heart of their Philosophy,[1] and which the modern

---

[1] Which Jung has incorporated in his interpretations of the human psyche.

scientist finds indispensable as an instrument in exploring nature. The Heracleitean system might be described as a 'dynamic equilibrium' and it is in such terms that science still describes the physical world. One example – from the physicists – must suffice. For some time physicists had begun to look at matter in a new way. When they found a new particle they straightway began to look for and expected to find its anti-particle. In 1959 Segré and Chamberlain working at Berkeley were awarded the Nobel Prize for having isolated the anti-proton. At the moment there appear to be numerous particles with their corresponding anti-particles. So the main ingredients of anti-matter – anti-protons, anti-neutrons, anti-electrons etc. – can be set in the tables alongside the protons, neutrons, electrons, etc., of which ordinary matter is composed. Much experiment and vast technological advance have taken place since Heracleitus compiled his table of opposites. But the approach is remarkably similar.[1]

Professor Karl Popper, who believes that it is important to convey to us something of the enthusiasm he feels for these pre-Socratic thinkers, has reduced Heracleitus' message to the profound and striking dictum that: MEN ARE FLAMES AND THINGS ARE PROCESSES. It was indeed an exciting book which the dropsical old man entrusted to Diana of the Ephesians; and she might have preserved it better.

[1] Since this paragraph was written, published results of certain experiments appear to have upset this neat symmetry of the physical world – for the time being, at any rate.

CHAPTER VII

Parmenides and Zeno of Elea

> Language cannot adequately describe reality unless
> the structure of the language is equivalent to the
> structure of the fact which it sets out to describe.
>
> WITTGENSTEIN

' "Cyclops," I said, "you wish to know the name I bear. I'll tell it you; and in return I should like to have the gift you promised me. My name is Nobody. That is what I am called by my mother and father and all my friends."

'The Cyclops answered me with a cruel jest. "Of all his company I will eat Nobody last, and the rest before him. That shall be your gift." '

At this point in the conversation, the Cyclops fell asleep, was blinded by the concerted effort of Odysseus and his men, and then by his howling brought all the other Cyclopes to the cave.

' "What on earth is wrong with you, Polyphemus? Why must you disturb the peaceful night and spoil our sleep with all this shouting? Is a robber driving off your sheep, or is somebody trying by treachery or violence to kill you?"

'Out of the cave came Polyphemus' great voice in reply: "O my friends, it's Nobody's treachery, no violence, that is doing me to death."

' "Well then," they answered, in a way that settled the matter, "if nobody is assaulting you in your solitude, you must be sick. Sickness comes from almighty Zeus and cannot be helped. All you can do is to pray to your father, the Lord Poseidon."

'And off they went, while I chuckled to myself at the way in which my happy notion of a false name had taken them in.'[1]

Odysseus outlived so many of his compeers who had fought with him on the windy plains of Troy because to physical strength and

[1] *The Odyssey*, Book IX (Penguin).

courage he allied a sophisticated cunning. He represents a more highly developed civilisation than do the Cyclopes. He knows well that his leadership and his right arm are realities, whatever name they go by, and that language was made by and for man, and not man for language. The Cyclopes, on the other hand, poor, brutish, barbarian souls, are taken in by the trick of calling somebody nobody, and so remain unaware of the realities of the situation.

Polyphemus and his deception may seem a far cry from Parmenides; but there is a parallel. Parmenides of Elea, in southern Italy, was in his prime some twenty years after Heracleitus, and had probably been educated by Pythagoreans. When he eventually formulated his own philosophy he set it forth in a volume of verse, fragments of which have survived. If his language and method seem strange to us, and his conclusions unlikely or even startling, we must not by any means underrate his importance in the chain of Greek thought. In his book he wrote:

> Come, I will tell you – and you must accept my word when you have heard it – the ways of enquiry which alone are to be thought: the one that IT IS, and it is not possible for IT NOT TO BE, is the way of credibility, for it follows Truth; the other, that IT IS NOT, and that IT is bound NOT TO BE: this I tell you is a path that cannot be explored; for you could not recognise that which IS NOT, nor express it.[1]

Parmenides is here trying out the fledgling wings of Logic, of pure reason, on the central problem of the time, the problem of change. He finds it perfectly logical and reasonable to postulate Being, or What-is, or the existence of the universe. When he says 'it is not possible for IT NOT TO BE', he means that empty space, nothingness or void is unthinkable and unutterable. Part of the difficulty here, as has been pointed out by writers about man's prehistory, is that in primitive thought, to name a thing was to create it; and to destroy a name was to destroy the thing to which it was attached. So the very act of naming NOTHING made it SOMETHING.

Next, if there was no void, there could be no movement, no change in the universe. For without void there was nowhere for things to originate from or to pass into. Not only is spatial movement and change denied but change in quantity and quality are ended. The entire universe is completely full (a plenum) and completely

[1] *Ancilla to the Pre-Socratic Philosophers*, p. 42, Fr. 2.

solid. That being the case, everything in it is indestructible and exists in a timeless moment, a Now.

This way of thinking, is, of course, diametrically opposed to that of Heracleitus, who in searching for a constant, found it in perpetual change. Parmenides banished change by a mental act and in his book instructed his followers to have nothing to do with Heracleitean heresy:

> But next I debar you from that way along which wander mortals knowing nothing, two-headed, for perplexity in their bosoms steers their intelligence astray, and they are carried along as deaf as they are blind, amazed, uncritical hordes, by whom TO BE and NOT TO BE are regarded as the same and not the same and (for whom) in everything there is a way of opposing stress.[1]

So Parmenides took the 'opposing stress', the mainspring, out of the Heracleitean universe and brought it to a standstill.

But change and opposing stress are not the only things banished by the Parmenidean poem. It goes on to say:

> For this (view) can never predominate, that That Which Is Not exists. You must debar your thought from this way of search, nor let *ordinary experience* in its variety force you along this way, (namely, that of allowing) the eye, sightless as it is, and the ear, full of sound, and the tongue, to rule; but (you must) judge by means of the *Reason* (Logos) the much contested proof which is expounded by me.[2]

It is clear, then, that experience, the search through the senses and empiricism (such as it may have been) are to yield to Logic.

ZENO

Also the two-edged tongue of Mighty Zeno, who,
Say what you would, could argue it untrue.

PLUTARCH (*Life of Pericles*)

Zeno was a pupil and staunch supporter of Parmenides. He too felt that the world was one and indivisible; he too felt that there was something baffling and hitherto unexplained about the phenomenon of motion. Zeno's favourite method was to accept the premises of his philosophical opponents and to show that they led to contradictory

[1] Ibid., p. 43, Fr. 6.   [2] Ibid., Fr. 7.

and so, impossible conclusions. It was this kind of argument which earned for him from Aristotle the title of inventor of dialectic. For example, by introducing the concept of infinite divisibility of things, Zeno 'proved' that if the One of Parmenides was not accepted, and if matter was composed of discrete units, as the Pythagoreans taught, these units would be at the same time 'both small and great: so small as to have no size, so large as to be infinite'.

Linked with Zeno's arguments against the concept of change, void and discrete particles, were his famous paradoxes concerning the possibility – or rather the impossibility – of motion:

1. THE DICHOTOMY (sometimes referred to as THE STADIUM). It is impossible to complete a race and get to the end of the stadium. For in order to complete the distance from point *A* to point *B* one must first complete half the distance between *A* and *B*, then half the remaining distance, then half the then remaining distance and so on *ad infinitum*. There is no end to this dichotomy and so there is no end to the race. Indeed it is worse than that: a moving object will never reach *any* given point because it must always complete first the half-way stage; so not only can a race not be finished – it can never begin.

2. THE ACHILLES. This paradox has the additional complication of a moving goal. In a race between Achilles and a tortoise (which is naturally given a handsome start) the hero can never overtake his rival. However fast he runs, Achilles must first reach the spot from which the tortoise started. By that time the tortoise will have drawn ahead. Achilles must then make up that distance and again the tortoise will have drawn ahead. We go on saying this *ad infinitum*. Achilles is always catching up, but he never actually overhauls the tortoise.

3. THE FLYING ARROW. The arrow in flight is at rest. For if everything is at rest when it occupies a space equal to itself, and what is in flight does at every given instant occupy a space equal to itself, it cannot move.

4. THE MOVING UNITS (often called THE STADIUM but not to be confused with No. 1). Suppose, as in the diagrams below, we have three rows of an equal number of equal units and of these rows one is stationary and two are moving with equal velocity in opposite directions. If we halt the process as in diagram 2 we find that in the

same time, the leader of the Bs has passed two As but four Cs. Zeno assumes that the time taken for any one unit to pass any other unit is a unit of time and he therefore concludes that the performance of the leading B proves that four is equal to two.

1	2
A A A A	A A A A
B B B B	B B B B
C C C C	C C C C

We can see now something of what was embodied in the popular opinion as recorded by Plutarch of 'Mighty Zeno, who, say what you would, could argue it untrue'. For if as a result of the first two paradoxes one decided that the possibility of infinite divisibility of space and time was unacceptable – and there were those who, later, took up just this point of view – then paradoxes three and four form the other horn of the dilemma to hedge one in. In the words of Sir Desmond Lee:

> The first two arguments, as we have seen, assume that space, and probably also time, are continuous and infinitely divisible. The third assumes that time is discontinuous and composed of indivisibles, and has a natural implication that space also is discontinuous. The fourth assumes that time consists of instants, as does the third, and that space consists of minimal extensions. The four in fact form a quartet of which the first two proceed on the assumption of infinite divisibility, the second two on that of indivisibles.[1]

If we revert to the first paradox and imagine a simple example of a course one mile in length, then the runner has to cover first half a mile, then one quarter, then one eighth and so on. He has to traverse distances represented by the series

$$\tfrac{1}{2}+\tfrac{1}{4}+\tfrac{1}{8}+\tfrac{1}{16}+\tfrac{1}{32}+\tfrac{1}{64}+ \ldots$$

His difficulty is that, stated in these terms, there is always just another little section of the track left to cover before he reaches the finishing tape. But students of mathematics know very well now that there is a 'limit' to the sum of an infinite geometric series such as this and that the sum of this series is 1. So there is an end to the race.

Again, if in the contest between Achilles and the tortoise we say

[1] Lee: *Zeno of Elea*, p. 102 (Cambridge).

that Achilles moves at ten times the speed of his rival and that he gives it a start of 100 yards, then while Achilles covers the first 100 yards the tortoise has travelled 10. While Achilles is covering this 10 yards the tortoise has moved on another yard, and so on. The distance covered by the tortoise in the race will be the sum to infinity of the series

$$10 + 1 + \tfrac{1}{10} + \tfrac{1}{100} + \tfrac{1}{1000} + \tfrac{1}{10000} + \cdots$$

And the sum of this series is $11\tfrac{1}{9}$ yards.

But although these answers are satisfactory for certain mathematical manoeuvres, they tell us rather where and when the races end rather than HOW IT HAS BEEN DONE. After all, what is the use of telling us that the sum of the infinite number of points in the first race is 1 when we know that we started off with a track one mile long? We must beware of thinking too easily 'that a "sum to infinity" is something real, and that the first two paradoxes are answered by taking the sum to infinity of a geometric series. For "sum to infinity" is a delicate mathematical concept. It is defined as the "limit of the sum to n terms as n tends to infinity". Although n tends to infinity, it never reaches it, by the definition of infinity. Accordingly, Zeno's problem remains.'[1]

To meet this difficulty, about one hundred years later, Xenocrates, who was a colleague of Aristotle's in Plato's Academy, decided that there must be atomic lengths which could not be subject to further division. Aristotle, on the other hand, held that all lengths are capable of infinite division but that Zeno ought to have decided to do one thing at a time: in other words, to run a race or to traverse a given distance is one thing; to engage in the process of dividing up a given distance is quite another. Let us look at a translation of his own words:

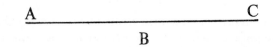

A   C

B

Take point A as the beginning, point C as the end, and a point B between them. This 'point between', as soon as we take it, divides AC into two, and itself constitutes an end with respect to A and a

[1] I am indebted to N. B. Booth for this note.

beginning with respect to *C*, and thus, while only single in place, it is double in function. We shall see that the distinction between potentiality and actuality also comes into play here, and so, whereas any point between the extremities may be made to function dually in the sense explained, it does not actually function unless the mobile actually divides the line by stopping and beginning to move again. . . . Accordingly, if we are asked whether it is possible to go through an unlimited number of points, whether in a period of time or in a length, we must answer that in one sense it is possible but in another not. If the points are actual it is impossible, but if they are potential it is possible.[1]

Now of course every Greek man and boy training in his city gymnasium knew that the conclusions forced on him by Zeno were outrageous and contrary to daily experience. But a good disciple of Parmenides could always argue: 'Your senses tell you that you can run to the end of the stadium and that the arrow can find its mark, but can you with your intellect, with your powers of reasoning, find a flaw in Zeno's arguments?' And this no one could do with any degree of certainty.

'But', it is commonly objected, 'if Parmenides and the Eleatics pushed to such lengths their monistic theory of the universe and their attack upon the five senses, why should we take them seriously?'

To begin with, many Greek thinkers were unhappy to some extent about the evidence of the senses. The stock examples used in casting doubt upon their validity were: the straight oar-blade which appeared bent in water; the honey which tasted sweet to most, but bitter to a man suffering from jaundice; the myriad motes and molecules seen cavorting about in the sun's rays when they streamed through a keyhole but otherwise invisible; the fire in the distant valley which appeared no bigger than a man's hand but was in reality quite large.

Now, Heracleitus had written that the eyes and ears were bad witnesses for men if they had 'barbarian souls'. And a barbarian was strictly one who spoke a language which a Greek did not understand. The word 'barbarian' simply means one who appears to be saying no more than *barbarbarbar*. . . . Just as it would be unreasonable for a Greek to assume that a Persian was talking nonsense because he could not understand his language, so it was unreasonable to assume

[1] Aristotle: *Physics*, Vol. II, Bk. VIII (Loeb Classical Library, Heinemann).

that the senses were false because man was, as yet, a mere infant or stranger in his converse with nature. Throughout the history of discovery it has proved more fruitful to give a fair hearing to the evidence of the senses than to suppress it.

In the instance of the bent oar-blade Heracleitus was interestingly vindicated. Something did bend on entering the water; but it was light and not the oar. One of the Ptolemies, just three hundred years later, was measuring the angles of incidence and refraction when light passed from air to water, from air to glass and from water to glass. He was unable, however, to discover the law relating to these angles. This discovery and the dissemination of it had to await Snell, of Holland, and Descartes working in another great period of bustling scientific advance.

Parmenides and Zeno introduced the concepts of 'plenum' and 'continuum' to their considerations of the whole of nature. The continuum was in direct contrast to the Pythagorean idea of a world composed of discrete points; the plenum was the alternative to the existence or possibility of void. From that time these terms have played a vital role in man's attempt to form an imaginative picture of his universe. When Huygens proved the wave nature of light, when Faraday described reality as a continuous field and when Clerk-Maxwell deduced the existence of electromagnetic waves travelling on an ubiquitous ether, they were describing in more specific and mathematical terms something of what the members of the Eleatic School had tried to state in terms of logic and linguistics. Parmenides denied dogmatically the existence of 'the void'. The concept of an ether sufficiently ubiquitous to penetrate the stoutest walls, sufficiently ubiquitous to transmit radio waves from the most distant star, could be a powerful argument in his favour.

But the ether itself was only a concept, and one which, as Einstein pointed out, would have to go if it did not square with observed facts. Now it has virtually gone. Knowledge appears to move forward in a series of claims and counter-claims; and so in spite of Parmenides' apparently perverse thinking, we must treat him with care. He and his School provided an important clue in the all-absorbing enquiry of the pre-Socratic Greeks into the nature of their universe – in the enquiry which culminated in the postulating of the atom.

Homer (and so many succeeding generations nurtured by him)

described the world in concrete and colourful episodes and images: Parmenides represents man beginning to describe the world in an abstract, conceptual way; and so confident was he in his method that when his reason and his experience were at odds, particularly with regard to change and motion (which was only another form of change), he took his stand by reason. Parmenides said: '*Either* IT IS *or* IT IS NOT.' Aristotle began to say: 'We must consider the possibility that IT IS *and* IT IS NOT.' This is precisely the attitude that man in exploring natural law has to adopt from time to time.

Zeno, in supplementing the arguments of his master, Parmenides, graphically demonstrated how true it is that man in his probing of natural law is constantly grappling with contradictions and paradox. Indeed we might almost say that if the fear of the Lord is the beginning of wisdom, the continued effort to solve some paradox is for man the beginning of knowledge.

But Zeno did more than that: he set men's minds to work on the problems of infinity. As E. P. Northrop writes in his book *Riddles in Mathematics*:

> For well over two thousand years mathematicians have been struggling with the infinite. They cannot afford to disregard it, for it is indispensable in much of their work. Yet in their attempts to understand it and use it, they have run up against many contradictions. Some of these they have been able to overcome, while others are still causing them trouble. Indeed, the paradoxes enunciated by Zeno of Elea in the fifth century B.C. have never been settled to the complete satisfaction of all mathematicians.[1]

Suggested Reading

Lee, H. D. P. *Zeno of Elea* (Cambridge).
Northrop, E. P. *Riddles in Mathematics* (Pelican). (Chapter 7, Paradoxes of the Infinite, deals with Zeno.)
Pedoe, D. *The Gentle Art of Mathematics* (E.U.P.).
Ryle, Gilbert. *Dilemmas* (Cambridge). (Particularly Chapter III, Achilles and the Tortoise.)

[1] p. 116 (Pelican).

CHAPTER VIII

Empedocles and Anaxagoras

Signposts to the Atom Country

But no, this heart will glow no more, thou art
A living man no more, Empedocles!
Nothing but a devouring flame of thought –
But a naked, eternally restless mind.

MATTHEW ARNOLD: *Empedocles on Etna*

So wrote Matthew Arnold of his Empedocles before making him leap from the lip of Etna's crater. By this leap – traditional rather than historical – Empedocles was reunited with the four elements which he, as philosopher-physicist, had postulated and popularised:

To the elements it came from
Everything will return.
Our bodies to Earth;
Our blood to Water;
Heat to Fire;
Breath to Air.[1]

Empedocles of Acragas, a town in Sicily, was one of those men possessed by a cosmic surge of energy and a seething curiosity. He swept round the island of Sicily like a 'devouring flame of thought' attracting legendary reputations as he went. That he was now dubbed a wizard with power to control the winds and now a god with power to raise the dead was no doubt because of his conviction that nature could be understood by man and partially controlled.

He bears a striking resemblance to Pythagoras in the versatility and the nature of his pursuits. An active political adviser, he was absorbed in the study of medicine and natural philosophy. Indeed, so strongly

[1] *Empedocles on Etna*, Act II.

was Empedocles imbued with Orphic mysticism and Pythagorean principles that a tradition arose which made him a renegade Pythagorean, expelled from the brotherhood for having divulged their teaching in his poems. Like the brotherhood he felt compelled to acknowledge the totem and taboo, to refrain from beans and bay-leaves, and sacrificial blood. In his belief in the process of reincarnation, he was as doctrinaire as the most orthodox Orphic. His own bald statement informs us that he has been born as 'boy, girl, plant, bird, and dumb sea fish'. In those final moments when this 'eternally restless mind' is about to end its incarnation as Empedocles of Acragas, Matthew Arnold expressed the soul's argument:

> And then we will unwillingly return
> Back to this meadow of calamity,
> This uncongenial place, this human life.
> And in our individual human state
> Go through the sad probation all again,
> To see if we will poise our life at last,
> . . .[1]

In his account of nature Empedocles took the rather pudding-like world of the Eleatics, Parmenides and Zeno, and modified it in the light of experience in such a way as to allow for change and movement. Not surprisingly, a preoccupation with human physiology and living organisms where the cycle of birth, growth and decay is all important made Empedocles think of the world and reality in dynamic terms. For him the whole created universe consists of four elements – or roots, as he called them – and two forces: Earth, Air, Fire and Water, and Love and Hate. All the manifold substances known to man are capable of ultimate reduction to these four elements; the diversity of materials and their disposition throughout the universe at any moment are the work of two forces; Love, the force of attraction, brings things together in an infinite number of arrangements, and Hate, the force of repulsion, causes them in turn to separate out. In this way, the Parmenidean principle that nothing is either created or destroyed is sustained. For any creature, Life is merely the combining of the elements which go to make it up, or 'the fitting together of the elements by rivets of Love' as Empedocles so poetically put it. Death is the separation of those same elements.

[1] Ibid.

Lest his readers should doubt that such diverse forms of life could emerge from so few elements Empedocles adds this illustration:

> As when painters decorate temple offerings with colours – men who, following their intelligence, are well skilled in their craft – these, when they take many-coloured pigments in their hands, and have mixed them in a harmony, taking more of some, less of another, create from them forms like to all things, making trees and men and women and animals and fish nurtured in water, and even long-lived gods, who are highest in honour. . . .[1]

Some twenty or thirty years later we find the atomists using a similar illustration.

Again like Pythagoras, Empedocles displayed an intellect of rare acuity in dealing with physical phenomena. As before we see at work the method of basing cosmic principle on particular, observed, domestic details in the everyday life of husbandman and housewife. In this way he discovered the corpuscular nature of air and light – a discovery which vitally affected his thinking on the nature of matter. In one of the longest passages preserved from his poem we find:

> The way everything breathes in and out is as follows: all creatures have tubes of flesh, empty of blood, which extend over the surface of the body; and at the mouths of these tubes the outermost surface of the skin is perforated with frequent pores, so as to keep in the blood while a free way is cut for the passage of air. Thus, when the thin blood flows back from here, the air, bubbling, rushes in in a mighty wave; and when the blood leaps up (to the surface), there is an expiration of air. As when a girl, playing with a water-catcher of shining brass – when, having placed the mouth of the pipe on her well-shaped hand she dips the vessel into the yielding substance of silvery water, still the volume of air pressing from inside on the many holes keeps out the water, until she uncovers the condensed stream (of air). Then at once when the air flows out, the water flows in in an equal quantity.[2]

The passage then goes on to explain that if the water-catcher is full of liquid and the hand is kept over the aperture at the top, atmospheric pressure, or as he calls it, 'the air outside, striving to get in', prevents the liquid from flowing out. This 'water-catcher' can be thought of as a rather capacious pipette which was used in Greek households for transferring quantities of liquid from one type of

---

[1] Freeman: *Ancilla*, p. 55, Fr. 23.   [2] Ibid., p. 62, Fr. 100.

vessel to another. It was used particularly for mixing water with wine.

One eminent writer of modern times took Empedocles to task for having formulated so foolish a theory of respiration when a few moments of quiet observation and reflection in his bath would have shown that there was no bubbling rush of air either in or out of the body's pores. This is a little unfair to Empedocles and would appear to miss an important point which he was trying to demonstrate: that all matter, while corporeal, consisted of tiny particles which were differently graded in different substances; and very fine particles could pass through pores where larger particles would be denied a passage. Therefore, since neither blood nor water were fine enough to pass through the pores, and no air would be available to the pores submerged in the bath-water, nothing would pass through them and there would be no bubbles.

Again using the principle of particles and pores Empedocles had some interesting things to say about the nature of light. In a passage in which he was attempting to explain the mechanism of the human eye we find this interesting simile:

> As when a man, thinking to make an excursion through a stormy night, prepares a lantern, a flame of burning fire, fitting lantern-plates to keep out every sort of winds, and these plates disperse the breath of the blowing winds; but the light leaps out through them, *in so far as it is finer*, and shines across the threshold with unwearying beams. . . .[1]

So the lantern-plates too (probably made of horn) are porous and the pores are of such a calibre as to permit the transmission of particles of light while restricting the particles of air. In another context Empedocles explained that not only did light consist of tiny particles but that these particles emanated from the area of the sun in the vault of heaven and travelled towards us at tremendous speed.

The conception of pores is vital to Empedocles' theory of matter. Although he would not have had magnifying lenses with which to examine them he would in his detailed study of plant and animal life have met with evidence for them in the manifold forms of exudation. When explaining how the four Elements and Love and Hate made up all the substances known to man, he used this expression: 'running

[1] Ibid., p. 60, Fr. 84.

GP E

through one another, they became now this, now that, and like things evermore'. In this way, too, growth was accounted for: the accretion of like substance to like because of the attraction of like for like. Aristotle commenting on this pointed out that Empedocles had in mind that the pores of like bodies would be symmetrical and of the same size and that this would facilitate the 'running through' and the 'mixing' by which matter is built up. With a certain touch of genius Empedocles formulated an extension to his theory of pores: that all matter, organic and inorganic, was constantly giving off emanations, and that by this 'giving off' matter was constantly being consumed. In this way he attempted to explain the attraction between magnet and iron: the emanations from the one were symmetrical with the pores of the other. Aristotle said that in his theory of the structure of matter Empedocles was almost an atomist without knowing it. We can see that he adumbrated too a theory of radiation and lattice structure which was to become important in the work of Democritus and modern crystallography.

As for the disposition of matter in the universe, Empedocles believed that a great whirl or vortex had been formed at a time when Hate had been dominant in all things. Since Hate was the force which caused a separating out of things, it had forced the Elements, Fire and Air, out to the limits of creation, thus forming the vault of heaven, sun, moon, fixed stars and planets. The humble nature of the similes used in describing his system can be seen embodied in the quotations extant: the vortex, the separating out and the fixing together of the universe were suggested by the actions which take place in the making of (1) cheese, (2) porridge, (3) pottery. That the heavenly bodies maintained their revolutions without falling caused no surprise after Empedocles had experimented with a cup of water whirled round on the end of a string.

As for the myriad creatures of this planet, they too come to birth and dissolution by the action of the forces of Love and Hate in conjunction with the four Elements. In his discussion of the development of life, although the evidence remaining is rather fragmentary, Empedocles adumbrated a theory of evolution to which was linked the idea of the survival of the fittest. He certainly believed that the earth had seen some very grotesque creatures and that the combinations arrived at were extremely haphazard. That all was for the best in the best of all possible worlds would have seemed as unrealistic to him as did some of the discarded by-products of the evolutionary forces. We must go no further here than to say 'adumbrated', for commentators are constantly cautioning us not to read the entire conclusions of Charles Darwin into the tentative probings of a naturalist – however brilliant – writing some twenty-three centuries earlier.

But it is not necessary to spoil our tribute to Empedocles by avoidable exaggeration. However retarded his age may have been in devising experimental techniques for enlarging the field of knowledge, there is no doubt that he was a thinker of power and originality whose dynamic concepts were similar in spirit to those of modern times. Professor Sambursky, writing from the standpoint of a modern philosopher-physicist, says this:

> ... Empedocles in his qualitative, poetic way was the first to postulate the reality of causes in the physical world and to identify them with forces. The modern physicist is amazed at the intuition which led Empedocles to propound the simultaneous existence of forces of attraction and repulsion. As far as our experience goes today, the physicist has been obliged to introduce forces of these two kinds. In opposition to the attractive force of gravitation there are cosmic forces of repulsion at work bringing about the expansion of the universe by the recession of the galaxies. In the atomic field we know of the positive and negative electric charges which repel those of the same kind and attract their opposites. And in nuclear physics too we cannot dispense with the assumption of repulsive and attractive forces.[1]

Shortly after his death a tradition gained currency that Empedocles had claimed godhead for himself and that his leap into the fiery furnace of Etna was a self-appointed act of apotheosis. More likely this was a too literal interpretation of his belief that knowledge is power and that the understanding of Nature involves identification with Nature. In the struggle towards this understanding he believed that the human senses were of paramount importance – provided, of course, they were not speaking to 'barbarian souls'. Indeed, so human was Empedocles that he regretted the power of the common cold in the head to impair the power of the senses from time to time, showing that not only had the Greeks a word for it, but that they had the thing itself – the accursed *coryza*.

[1] *The Physical World of the Greeks*, p. 19 (Routledge).

Anaxagoras – alias 'Old Nous'.

It's a very odd thing –
As odd as odd can be –
That whatever Miss T eats
Turns into Miss T.
WALTER DE LA MARE

'Man ist was er isst.'
(*Man is what he eats.*)
FEUERBACH

Anaxagoras was the first of the major philosophers to settle in Athens and was also the first to suffer because of his rationalist views. He came from an Ionian town to Athens in the year of Salamis where he lived until his expulsion for impiety thirty years later. Thus he was contemporary with the great men: Aeschylus, Sophocles, Euripides and Pericles, and on the latter two had a notable influence. The main burden of the charge of impiety was his teaching that the sun and moon were not, after all, gods, but large chunks of incandescent rock. In the words of Sir James Jeans, 'the average Greek was very loth to exchange his friendly and tutelar deities for inanimate masses of molten metal'. So Anaxagoras left perforce for Lampsacus on the Dardanelles where he continued to teach until his death, the anniversary of which the schoolchildren – thereby showing better sense than the adults of Athens – kept sacred as a holiday. But then Lampsacus was a colony of Miletus.

Philosophically speaking, Anaxagoras could not stomach the all too solid Parmenidean pudding. Like Empedocles, he agreed with Parmenides in denying the existence of a vacuum and the possibility of things 'coming into being' or 'passing away'. But also like Empedocles he realised that some satisfactory explanation must be found for the kaleidoscopic changes in nature and for the never-ending transmutation of one substance into another. His approach to the Milesian question was centred mainly on the problem of metabolism and growth. How did it come about that porridge, bread, figs and wine turned into bones, blood, flesh and hair? What account of matter would satisfactorily explain how the cow feeding in the pasture produced nourishing, gleaming-white milk, while the serpent in the same pasture produced a liquid that was dark and lethal? In a fragment from his book we find the words: 'How can hair come from not-hair, and flesh from not-flesh?'[1]

We know from what remains of his book what answer Anaxagoras gave to his own question. Just as Zeno in his paradox said that sections of a race-course were capable of being divided up *ad infinitum* and that after each division there would always be a tiny bit of space to cover, so Anaxagoras held that bits of matter were capable of infinite division without the particles disappearing. For if a point was reached where there was nothing left to divide further, it would have meant that matter had disappeared, that 'something' had become 'nothing'; but that this was impossible was taken as axiomatic by all. Within a generation Leucippus and Democritus had called a halt to this process of infinite division by their assertion that ultimately one came down to a particle which was not capable of further division – at least not PHYSICALLY. This particle was, of course, the **atom**; and the Greek word *atomos* simply means 'that which cannot be cut'. In the course of his argument Anaxagoras accustomed men to think in terms of particles infinitely small and far beyond the limits of human perception.

Having established that matter exists in quantities infinitesimal, in answer to the question 'How can hair come from not-hair, and flesh from not-flesh?' Anaxagoras said, 'In everything there is a portion of everything.' So that a grain of wheat or a grain of flour contains within it what he called 'seeds' of flesh, bone, blood and hair; and so the digestive process was simply the 'separating out' of the seeds of each thing and adding like to like. Of course we do not see all these elements when we look at a grain of wheat because in wheat the seeds of wheat are uppermost, predominant, and the seeds of the other things are totally invisible to the human eye. Lucretius, the greatest Roman exponent of the atomic system, had this to say by way of refuting Anaxagoras:

> He asserts that there is in everything a mixture of everything, but all the ingredients escape detection except the one whose particles are most numerous and conspicuous and lie nearest the surface. This is far removed from the truth. Otherwise, it would naturally happen that corn, when it is crushed by the dire force of the grind-stone would often show some sign of blood, and that blood would exude when we crush between stones any of those

[1] Freeman: *Ancilla*, p. 84, Fr. 19.

things that derive material from our bodies. Similarly, grass and water ought often to emit sweet drops of the same flavour as milk in the udders of fleecy ewes. When clods of soil are crumpled, finely divided particles of different plants and grains and leaves ought to become visible, lurking among the soil. When sticks are snapped, ashes and smoke ought to be revealed, and tiny hidden fires. But observation plainly shows that none of these things happens. It is clear therefore that one sort of thing is not intermingled with another in this way. . . .[1]

So clearly Lucretius understood Anaxagoras to mean that any given piece of matter such as a grain of corn, a clod of earth or a stick, contained within it the seeds – infinitely small – of all other substances. It was precisely to make this a credible hypothesis that he had first postulated the existence of matter in inconceivably small quantities.

All these early Greek philosophers felt called upon to explain the phenomenon of movement in their universe; movement of man and moon, sea and sun, flame and flower. Usually they associated movement with divinity; Thales had said there were gods in everything – in so far as everything moved (for the most part this applied to the organic world, though it was realised that there must be a touch of the divine in the magnet); the Athenians worshipped the heavenly bodies as deities partly because of their regular movements; Anaximander, Heracleitus and Empedocles postulated some kind of cosmic force as the generator of movement. Like Empedocles, Anaxagoras believed that some primal power had set in motion a vortex which, acting upon the great amorphous mass of our universe, had set in train the 'coming together' and the 'separating out' which have produced things as we know them. To fulfil the role of this primal power he elected Nous or mind. Although he called it Nous, he wrote about it much in the way that men write about godhead:

> For it (Mind) is the finest of all things, and the purest, and has complete understanding of everything, and has the greatest power. All things which have life, both the greater and the less, are ruled by Mind. Mind took command of the universal revolution, so as to make things revolve at the outset. And the things which were mixed together, and separated off, and divided, were all understood by Mind.

[1] *The Nature of the Universe*, trs. R. E. Latham, Bk. I (Penguin).

In everything there is a portion of everything except Mind; and some things contain Mind also.[1]

Socrates, in his last conversation on earth – according to Plato's dialogue the *Phaedo* – took Anaxagoras to task for having dragged Mind into his system merely to impart motion to things. Socrates believed that anyone who introduced Mind into the universe must logically proceed to unfold the plan and purpose of that Mind. Socrates further believed that the plan would be the best possible for man and that the purpose of life was to seek it out and live by it. He was therefore disgusted to find that Anaxagoras assigned no greater part to Mind than that of the lash in a boy's hand which, heedless of what it is doing, keeps a top spinning. But Socrates and Anaxagoras were not pursuing the same enquiry. Anaxagoras was replying to the Ionian question about our nature and our origin. Socrates was perpetually asking how man – since he had arrived – should behave in society and how he should find and fulfil the purpose for which he had arrived. And, in the main, Socrates was quite as lacking in curiosity about the Ionian question as were the Ionians about his.

It is often interesting to note the striking similarity of thought between these Ionians and modern scientists. Any gap there is, is one of techniques and means of measurement, of telescopes, microscopes and radio waves. Today scientists – in America at least – are scanning the heavens for radio signals from other inhabited worlds which they feel sure exist somewhere on those far-flung limbs of spiralling nebulae. By the year 400 B.C. any Athenian could purchase for one drachma Anaxagoras' book *On Natural Science* which told him that the great cosmic rotation set up by Nous had thrown off other worlds than his and that these worlds had each their own sun and moon.

[1] Freeman: *Ancilla*, p. 84, Fr. 11, 12.

CHAPTER IX

The Atomists

... for it seem'd
A void was made in Nature; all her bonds
Crack'd; and I saw the flaring atom-streams
And torrents of her myriad universe,
Ruining along the illimitable inane,
Fly on to clash together again, and make
Another and another frame of things
For ever.

TENNYSON: *Lucretius*

May reason rather than the event itself
convince you that the whole world can
collapse with one ear-splitting crack.

LUCRETIUS: *Bucinator Temporis Atomi*

Democritus said he would rather discover one law of nature than be the Great King of the whole Persian Empire. He had his wish: for not only was he known as The Encyclopaedia and The Laughing Philosopher in his own time, but now, almost two thousand four hundred years after he expressed the wish, the Greek government on the opening of its first atomic power-station has issued a postage stamp bearing his likeness and name, thus ascribing to him the most momentous discovery in the history of natural philosophy.

There was a tradition that Plato wished to have all the writings of Democritus assembled and burned. If that was so, he too had his wish in so far as no complete volume of Democritus has survived and almost certainly all his writings were first assembled, and later burned in the magnificent Museum of Alexandria. The Museum Library was fired once by the Christians and once by the Moslems. In this, succeeding generations suffered enormous loss; for Democritus was one of the most vigorous, voluminous and original writers which his, or any other age, has produced. Possessed by an insatiable curiosity for scientific detail he attempted to embrace and systematise the whole range of human knowledge. And at the centre of all was his atomic theory of matter.

Although Democritus was the major figure associated with an atomic theory of the universe, he was not the originator of that theory. That honour must go to Leucippus, a man who was in his prime about the year 430 B.C., and who wrote a major work entitled *The Great World-Order*. As with Homer, a number of cities appeared as rival claimants as the birth-place of Leucippus: the most important of these were Abdera – which was Democritus' city – and Miletus. Although it is of no real importance, one likes to think that the great question with which philosophy was introduced to Europe by Thales, Anaximander and Anaximenes was answered by a man of their own city.

It was Leucippus who boldly and with originality reconciled the champions of change with those of a rigid immobility, who resolved the dilemma between the protagonists of Pluralism and those who affirmed that the universe was One. What the stiff logic of Parmenides and the Eleatics refused to do; what the dynamic imagination of Empedocles could not quite achieve; what the magisterial Aristotle would not allow; that Leucippus did: he made a gap in nature. He knew that there was matter; he knew it moved, it was subject to change. But if matter and change were part of reality, then so was empty space. What-is-not could and must exist as surely as what-is; and if language and logic had not found a way of expressing such a possibility, so much the worse for language and logic. So great was the influence of Aristotle that even at the dawn of the modern world, as though Leucippus and his successors had never existed, Shakespeare was writing:

> . . . and Antony,
> Enthron'd in the market place, did sit alone,
> Whistling to the air; which, but for vacancy,
> Had gone to gaze on Cleopatra too,
> And made a gap in nature.[1]

Before discussing the form in which the theory appeared and its implications for the Greeks we must introduce the final member of

[1] *Antony and Cleopatra*, Act II, Sc. 2.

the atomic triumvirate. Epicurus, who settled in Athens towards the end of the following century and who founded the philosophy which bears his name, based his doctrines on the works of Democritus. Epicurus was primarily interested in formulating a faith for man to live by in troubled times. Although neither physicist nor mathematician, by his consistent reasoning and his will to create an ethical system, he modified the earlier atomic theory in some very important respects. Although his writings were buried and lost beneath the ruins of antiquity, his creed survived. His ardent disciple, the Roman, Titus Lucretius Carus, contemporary of Caesar and Cicero, embodied in his splendid hexameters the whole Epicurean doctrine. The *De Rerum Natura* is imbued with the urgency and interest of a philosopher-poet convinced of being the mouth-piece of a philosophy capable of liberating his fellow citizens from the malaise of their time. Materialist that he was, he called upon the Muse; and, materialist though he was, she came.

The basic facts then for the men who interpreted the universe in terms of atoms and void were these:

1. All reality can be reduced to a basic, underlying stuff – the atom.
2. Mathematically the atom is divisible; but physically it is indivisible, completely solid, unchangeable and indestructible. It is, in fact, the Parmenidean One in miniature.
3. All atoms are the same in substance – there is no other primary matter.
4. Variety is made by (*a*) their shape, (*b*) their arrangement, (*c*) their position.
5. Between atoms and between particles of matter there are intervals of empty space.
6. The atoms are infinite in number and the space is infinite in extent.
7. Atoms are eternally in motion – whether independently of each other or when linked together to form compound substances.
8. According to Epicurus, at least, atoms have weight. There is a very large but not infinite variety of shapes. There is an upper and lower limit to the size of atoms; they are never small enough to invite destruction; they are never large enough to be seen.

Plato (and his Academy) thought that this way of looking at the universe was too unholy to be tolerated (or it may have been that he saw in it too serious a challenge to his own system); Aristotle and the Lyceum looked upon it as an aberration. We, today, can see that in terms of discovering reality, it is the period of history begun by Plato and Aristotle, ending with Gassendi and Newton which might more aptly be termed the aberration. Indeed one might fairly be allowed no small degree of wonder when one considers how small was the gap in world outlook which separated Democritus from a physicist at the end of the last century.

How then did the Greeks arrive at this concept, virtually deprived as they were of the means of controlled experiment and so many centuries before what one American physicist has described as the 'world of brass and glass and wax and mercury and coils and lenses and vacuum pumps – above all a world of electronic amplifiers and photo-electric tubes'? The route by which they arrived is itself an excellent example of the continuity of thought and of the dialectic movement which they themselves had, in so many instances, taught.

Thales and the succeeding Ionians, Anaximander, Anaximenes and Heracleitus asserted that for all its manifold diversity, the world was ONE. Philosophers have called them Monists. Pythagoras and his brotherhood put forward the counter notion that the world consisted of discrete points. They were known as Pluralists. Parmenides and the Eleatics adopted the altogether extreme position that the universe was a completely solid, eternally changeless and unmoveable plenum. Further than that Monism could not go; and the famous Parmenidean One quickly found a niche in the history of philosophy. Next appeared Empedocles with his limited Pluralist ideas consisting of four elements and two forces, supported by Anaxagoras who said, 'In everything is a portion of everything.' Further than that Pluralism could not go. Finally, though not, of course, for ever, Leucippus stilled the wheel of controversy with a synthesis which has lasted till the present day. His atoms were such as the most militant Monists could demand; and they answered Anaxagoras, for they were the infinite seeds of creation.

But Ixion's wheel is never still. The comforting synthesis of yesterday gives rise to the uncertain thesis and antithesis of today. The Democritean atom, in laboratories from Germany to Japan has recently been spawning particles at a bewildering speed. We now have electrons, positrons and neutrinos, protons and neutrons, and different kinds of mesons. As we mentioned in connection with Heracleitus, some of these particles have their associated anti-particles, though for the most part these are, as yet, hypothetical. Some of these particles have a lifetime so short that they mean little to the layman. So the neat little nuclear world as described by Democritus is disintegrating and posing fresh problems.

How then did Leucippus construct his cosmos and Epicurus his ethics on the basis of the atom? They held that all creation, growth, decay and destruction were but forms of atomic combination and dissolution. The whole of the infinite universe was full of atoms in motion. From time to time and in various parts of this universe a whirl or vortex – such as we have met before – is set up. The atoms, according to their various shapes, begin to interlock; fine particles are squeezed out to the fringes of the vortex; heavy particles move towards the centre and a cosmos is formed. This process is being acted and re-enacted all the time in all parts of the infinite so that there are always worlds such as ours in varying degrees of growth and dissolution. As far as Leucippus and Democritus were concerned this primal movement of the atoms was in all directions and was governed by natural law. Events and movements which appear to mortals as haphazard and the outcome of merest chance are governed by this natural law which is supreme throughout the universe. They banished Empedocles' forces of Love and Hate; they banished Anaxagoras' Mind; above all they banished any idea of a design or purpose from the entire scheme of things, and could not admit any kind of religious or mystical causation. In this, of course, they were anathema to Plato and Aristotle whose systems were highly teleological (the Greek word *telos* means an end or goal). Plato in particular would have been horrified at the thought of the 'argument from design' – one of the stock arguments in favour of a divinely appointed world – being demolished by Democritus, just as Victorian religion was shocked at its demolition by Darwin.

As far as we can see, it did not worry Democritus that his system was thoroughly deterministic and allowed no place for the operation of free will. Yet he was deeply concerned with ethics and problems of behaviour. It was here that Epicurus, who was primarily at pains to devise an effective, workaday philosophy, introduced his famous modification to the theory of the movement of the atoms. A thorough-going consistency was the hall-mark of Epicurus' thought and he knew it was idle to incorporate counsels of right behaviour in a system which did not admit of free will. Lucretius has put it with force and clarity:

'In this connection there is another fact that I want you to grasp. When the atoms are travelling straight down through empty space by their own weight, *at quite indeterminate times and places they swerve* ever so little from their course, just so much that you can call it a change of direction. If it were not for this swerve, everything would fall downwards like raindrops through the abyss of space. No collision would take place, and no impact of atom on atom would be created. Thus nature would never have created anything.'[1]

Again:

'Granted, then, that empty space extends without limit in every direction and that seeds innumerable in number are rushing on countless courses through an unfathomable universe under the impulse of perpetual motion, *it is in the highest degree unlikely that this earth and sky is the only one to have been created* and that all those particles of matter outside are accomplishing nothing. This follows from the fact that our world has been made from nature through the spontaneous and casual collision and the multifarious, accidental, random and purposeless congregation and coalescence of atoms whose suddenly formed combinations could serve on each occasion as the starting point of substantial fabrics – earth and sea and sky and the races of living creatures. On every ground, therefore, you must admit that there exist elsewhere other congeries of matter similar to this one which the ether clasps in its ardent embrace.'[2]

Since in common with all other creation, man – body, mind and soul – is made up of atoms, if all movement of these atoms were subject to Natural Law, man would be reduced to an automaton. It was to avoid this that Epicurus introduced the 'indeterminate swerve'. This 'swerve' on the part of the very fine atoms composing the mind enables them to slip out from the noose of the Natural Law and to take part in acts of volition.

Both Democritus and Epicurus taught that the atoms were eternally in motion. They agreed too that they were no more called upon to account for the cause of this eternal motion than they were to account for the existence of the atoms in the first place.

[1] *The Nature of the Universe*, Book II (Penguin).   [2] Ibid.

They well knew that an attempt to do so would involve them in one of those regressions unto infinity which achieve nothing. We have more specific evidence of Epicurus' views on this atomic movement so we shall follow him rather than Democritus here.

Epicurus convinced himself quite independently of his predecessors that a vacuum could exist. His simple observation and far-reaching conclusions based on them are in line with others mentioned above. He pointed out that if you brought two plates together and then separated them at great speed a vacuum was created. He pointed out further that light travelling from the sun every morning to illumine the world traversed the intervening atmosphere with very considerable velocity. Taking into account then that air was no mean resistant – Empedocles and Anaxagoras had demonstrated this by jumping on inflated bladders – Epicurus arrived at the conclusion that not only would atoms fall at tremendous speed in a vacuum, but that bodies, irrespective of weight, would fall at equal speed. It is both relevant and interesting to note here that Epicurus was well on the way towards the solution of the stock Greek problem of the 'oar bent in water' when he pointed out that the speed of light was altered on passing from one medium into another. It is also interesting that in the whole panorama of Greek philosophy there was no such consistent and determined champion of the validity of the senses as Epicurus.

Not only were the atoms in perpetual motion but they were constantly colliding with each other. These collisions in no way impaired the speed of the atoms, which always move in space at a speed which we may call 'atomic' and which we may visualise as 'the speed of thought'. But the direction of the atoms is altered by the blows, and the direction in which they fly off after each collision is determined by the angle of incidence. Here we have the atomists of antiquity conjuring up in the mind's eye just such a picture as Lord Rutherford and his team recorded with the assistance of photographic plates. In 1911 they directed a fusillade of fast-moving alpha particles (the nuclei of the helium atoms) through a dense layer of gas and found that most of the projectiles passed clean through the atoms of gas without striking anything. Some, however, were deflected from their course through very wide angles. In the following year they carried out a similar experiment substituting a sheet of thin gold foil for the layer of gas. Not only were some of the particles scattered through more than a right angle; some rebounded straight back in the direction of their source. 'It was almost as incredible', said Rutherford, 'as if you fired a fifteen-inch shell at a piece of tissue paper, and it came back and hit you.' The Greeks had said there was empty space between atom and atom; Rutherford showed that the atom itself was largely composed of empty space. The Greeks had said the atom was extremely minute: the precise measurements have now been made. The Greeks said it was immensely hard and indestructible: Rutherford's words above throw some light on the degree of hardness; but the splitting of an atomic nucleus by Cockcroft and Walton in 1932 made the name 'atom' an anachronism from that date. We can see now that much of what the Greeks said of their atom applies more accurately to what we now know as the elementary particles of the atom.

But what of the kaleidoscopic variety of the tangible, visible world? How did these countless millions of dull, identical (as far as substance went) atoms account for the world's wealth of sensory and spiritual experience? If the atom was without colour, how did one explain the evening sky over Ithaca during sunset? Or the morning light on the sea at Sunium as it dashed against the rocky cliffs and shimmered with a multitude of hues? How could that-which-had-no-colour produce the gaudy spectrum of the peacock's tail and the splendid sheen of Tyrian purple dye? Whence came the odour of the scented lotus or the Arabian myrrh, the flavour of honey from Hymettus and the joy of Rhodian wine? And if reality was reduced to insentient atoms and void, whence came man's power to perceive and pass judgment on these things?

The atomists were clear in their answer. The atoms were homogeneous in substance and in themselves devoid of colour, taste, smell and feeling. Their sole properties were size, weight and shape. Variety perceived by man arose from the different shapes, arrangements and positions of the atoms. As Aristotle later pointed out in relating the theory, the noblest or the meanest book is composed of the same letters of the alphabet set down in some of their possible arrangements. In the same way, the manifold creations of the universe were constructed of atoms in some of their different possible arrangements. Atoms of fire were spherical: this permitted extreme mobility. Atoms of smoke had hooked tentacles which produced irritation on sensitive membranes. Honey atoms were relatively round and smooth, vinegar atoms were relatively rough, and so each substance aroused different reactions from the tongue. So too, the colours of the seething waters at the cliff's edge, the colours of the peacock's tail arose from differences of shape, position and arrangement of the atoms.

Since atoms are eternally in motion throughout the boundless universe, they constantly coalesce to form compounds; but the speed and motion of the restless atoms are in no way diminished. Within the new-formed aggregate they are dancing to and fro in rapid collision and recoil. The compound body may appear to be stationary or to be moving uniformly in one direction, but always taking place within it and beyond the range of human vision are the feverish palpitations of the component atoms; 'As', says Lucretius, 'when a distant flock of grazing sheep appear motionless on a green hillside or a far-off company of men appear to move uniformly across the dusty plain.'[1]

Leucippus and Epicurus formulated quite clearly the novel and fertile idea that compound bodies were not merely aggregates of atoms but were new entities displaying qualities and faculties which individual atoms did not possess. The aggregate which we call water has the quality of 'wetness' though individual atoms have not. The aggregate which we call wine displays qualities of colour, taste and smell which individual atoms lack. Further, to account for all reality, including perceptual and emotional experience, they had to and they did extend this principle to embrace not only all the qualities of the world external to man, but also man's mental, emotional and spiritual experience. Mind and soul were aggregates of extremely fine and mobile atoms variously distributed throughout the body. Thought was defined as the motion set up in these atoms by stimulus from without. For Epicurus, at any rate, judgment and decision were possible by virtue of the indeterminate movement on the part of the atoms comprising the mind, which, like all atoms in the universe, are eternally in motion and capable of that unpredictable 'swerve' already mentioned.

Commentators are frequently at pains to warn readers not to impose modern implications on the relatively imprecise and speculative theories of the pre-Socratic philosophers – and rightly so. But there is an equal danger that, in the midst of the twentieth-century ex-

[1] Ibid.

plosion of experiment and calculation, regard for imagination and the historical approach may suffer neglect. It is primarily the technical ability to perform experiment and to devise methods of measurement which separates the physicist of today from Democritus. Ironically, it was the poet who was consciously anti-Science, Yeats, who summed up this difference when he wrote: 'Measurement began our might.'

Physicists today, in their investigation of matter, have reached an impasse. The fundamental units of matter behave at one moment as though they were particles and at another as though they were waves. Sir William Bragg used to say of X-rays that they were to be regarded as waves on Mondays, Wednesdays and Fridays, and as particles on Tuesdays, Thursdays and Saturdays.

Not only has physics been faced with this wave-particle duality, but it appears that a dilemma has arisen in the matter of observing experimentally the behaviour of fundamental particles (e.g. electrons) beyond a certain point. In order that a particle may be observed, it must be illuminated. But illumination is a form of energy the impact of which on the particle distorts its behaviour and diminishes the truth of our picture.

> Like following life thro' creatures you dissect,
> You lose it in the moment you detect.[1]

So that notwithstanding the experiments, the microscopes and the mathematics, science still has need of its Leucippus or its Democritus, its men of vision capable of making the bold imaginative leap in order to resolve the dilemma. For Leucippus it was the conflict between Monism and Pluralism; for us it has been the conflict between the wave-nature and the particle-nature of the elementary units of matter. The common bond linking the pioneers of atomism with their incomparably better equipped counterparts of today is that, in the end, both extend man's vision of reality in proportion to their success in constructing from experience an imaginative model of the universe which works.

[1] Pope: *Moral Essays*, Epistle I.

SUGGESTED READING

Asimov, Isaac. *Inside the Atom* (Abelard-Schuman).
Bailey, Cyril. *The Greek Atomists and Epicurus* (Oxford). (A large-scale, detailed work).
Lucretius. *The Nature of the Universe* (De Rerum Natura) (Penguin).

CHAPTER X

Athens - Sparta - City States

Self-love forsook the path it first pursued,
And found the private in the public good.
Thus God and nature linked the general frame,
And bade self-love and social be the same.

POPE: *Essay on Man*

The word 'pre-Socratic' has more than a mere chronological meaning. It denotes a way of looking at the world. Democritus, pinnacle of pre-Socratic thought, was, after all, nine or ten years younger than Socrates, and although many of his recorded sayings could have come from the lips of Socrates, between the two there is a great gulf fixed.

The word 'Socratic' too demands a brief explanation at the outset. Socrates wrote nothing. He indulged to the full one of the most treasured, most characteristic and most civilised of the arts of the Athenians: the art of talking. But his young admirer and fellow citizen Plato was a voluminous writer and made Socrates the central figure of almost all his many dialogues. And since Plato was a highly imaginative artist we can never be absolutely certain what the historical Socrates was like. So when we mention Socrates as doing or saying something, we ought to exercise the mental reservation: 'Socrates as portrayed by Plato'.

It is with the arrival of Socrates on the Athenian scene that a considerable change becomes apparent in the atmosphere of Greek thought. There is a marked shift of emphasis away from the study of nature by man towards the study of man in relation to nature and particularly that part of nature which we call society. What is new in Socrates' way of thinking is that he is primarily concerned with ethics, the study of man's behaviour in society, and theology, which deals with man's relationship to the divine. Such considerations actively involve the idea of purpose in life, or teleology. The impetus created by Socrates was caught up with tremendous zeal and power by Plato and Aristotle and infused by them into medieval and subsequent European thought.

A claim to account for this change and for Socrates' and Plato's systems of philosophy might be idle and presumptuous. But, at any rate, it is possible to point out that a very great historical movement was taking place in Greece, which certainly had a great deal to do with the change in attitudes on the part of the outstanding minds of the time. One age – the Classical – was drawing to a close; a new age – the Hellenistic – was about to be born. The Classical age is essentially associated with the Greek city states. The decline of the city-state system with all that it meant for citizen-Greeks played an enormous part in fixing that gulf between Democritus and Plato.

When Shakespeare was writing *Antony and Cleopatra* he was dealing with the change from one historical period to another. On hearing that Antony, the embodiment of the past, is dead, Augustus Caesar, the embodiment of the future, says:

> The breaking of so great a thing should make
> A greater crack.

That could not be said of the 'breaking' of the fifth-century polity of Greece in, for example, Athens and Sparta. The crack was immense and terrifying. Early Greek philosophy moves towards it in a spirit of confidence – for it does not know the future; post-Socratic philosophy is uniformly a movement of recoil. And since, as Shakespeare writes, again in *Antony and Cleopatra*

> I see men's judgments are
> A parcel of their fortunes, and things outward
> Do draw the inward quality after them.

we must now look as briefly as possible at the significant fortunes of the two city states – Athens and Sparta. We must look at both; for, poles apart, each was outstanding in its own way. And while Socrates and Plato lived and taught in the one, they appeared to be enamoured of the other.

There is a beautiful legend relating to the birth of Athens as a city. The gods were to compete with one another to see, with Zeus as arbiter, which one would make the fairest gift to the emergent city and consequently, as god-father or god-mother, assume the role of presiding deity. Poseidon's gift – according to one version – was the horse; Athene's the gentle olive tree. And although judgment was given for the goddess, whose olive groves thenceforth were sacred and whose name the city from that time has borne, Poseidon with horse and ship, in peace and war was closely linked with Athens. That the Athenians themselves were acutely conscious of the part played in their national life by these associations is brought out clearly in a beautiful translation of a beautiful ode of the tragic poet Sophocles in his play *Oedipus at Colonus*, produced in Athens when Socrates was nearing his death and Plato was an impressionable young man.

> Here in our white Colonus, stranger guest,
> Of all earth's lovely lands the loveliest,
> Fine horses breed, and leaf-enfolded vales
> Are thronged with sweetly-singing nightingales,
> Screened in deep arbours, ivy, dark as wine,
> And tangled bowers of berry-clustered vine;
> To whose dark avenues and windless courts
> The Grape-god with his nursing-nymphs resorts.
>
> Here Aphrodite rides with golden reins;
> The Muses here consort; and on these plains,
> A glory greater than the Dorian land
> Of Pelops own, or Asiatic strand,
> Our sweet grey foster-nurse, the olive, grows
> Self-born, immortal, unafraid of foes;
> Young knaves and old her ageless strength defies
> Whom Zeus and Pallas guard with sleepless eyes.
>
> And last, our Mother-city's chiefest pride
> I yet must praise, all other gifts beside,
> Poseidon's gift, which makes her still to be
> Mistress of horses, mistress of the sea.
> Here in these lanes wild horses first obeyed
> The bit and bridle; here the smooth oar-blade
> In slim and handy shape first learned to leap
> And chase the fifty sea-maids through the deep.[1]

One would hardly think that when Sophocles, himself a native of 'white Colonus', a suburb of Athens, wrote these words his city

[1] Trs. E. F. Watling (Penguin).

was nearing the end of a fearfully bloody and protracted war with 'the Dorian land of Pelops' – Sparta and her allies. Athens was defeated and, for a time at any rate, ceased to be 'mistress of horses, mistress of the sea'. We must cast a rapid glance over the events which led to this situation and at the nature of the two protagonists.

In 498 B.C. when Miletus was fighting for its liberty against the powerful Persian empire, the Athenians, who believed that they were akin to the Ionians, sent a squadron of ships to assist them. The revolt of Miletus from Persia was unsuccessful and its people suffered the final doom of death and deportation. But the Athenians had brought themselves to the notice of King Darius who resolved to put this small, impudent people in its place. The might of Persia marched and sailed to Europe in successive campaigns and returned to Asia leaving such names as Marathon, Thermopylae and Salamis as recompense to Greece for her losses in men and material, temples and towns. It was during the second of these invasions, prior to the battle of Salamis, that the Athenians took refuge in their ships, evacuating their city which was captured and destroyed by the Persians. The time had now passed when

> the smooth oar-blade
> In slim and handy shape first learned to leap
> And chase the fifty sea-maids through the deep.

As Herodotus, the historian of the war against Persia, pointed out, those twenty ships sent by Athens to assist the militant population of Miletus were the pursuers of trouble between Greek and barbarian.

When the barbarian flood retreated, Athens found herself the moral and material leader of a maritime league formed to protect the Aegean city states from any diminution of their liberty at the hands of Xerxes and his successors. By virtue of her seamanship and her adventurous response to challenge, she had taken her affairs at a flood tide upon which she was to ride for the best part of the century. Sparta had been invited to attend at Miletus and Marathon and had absented herself from both.

The degree to which Athens was converted from the natural leader of freely participating members of a maritime league to the demanding metropolis of an exploited and subject empire may be variously argued from the statistics available. That she did undergo such a change is a historical fact. By the middle of the fifth century,

Athens, splendidly adorned and rebuilt, now at her peak under the expansionist policy of Pericles, began to attract the jealousy of her economic rivals and the hatred of those who were either politically opposed or subject to her. In 431 B.C. matters came to a head with the outbreak of the Peloponnesian War which ended with the surrender of a humiliated and exhausted Athens, now deprived of empire and fleet, in 404 B.C.

The course of the war was punctuated by a number of appalling outbursts of bloodshed and severity. Thucydides, an Athenian general turned historian, in the third book of his account of the war records the hideous deterioration in standards of human behaviour. In every part of the Greek world touched by the struggle, values which civilised men had with difficulty established were reversed; the very meaning of words changed. 'Love of power', he writes, 'operating through greed and through personal ambition was the cause of all these evils, ... those who were least remarkable for intelligence showed the greater powers of survival. ... Ordinary conventions of civilised life were thrown into confusion.'[1]

Two episodes in the course of the conflict we must consider a little more closely. In the early years of the war, the city of Mytilene in the island of Lesbos revolted from Athens. The city was invested and captured by an Athenian fleet and army, and the Assembly met in Athens to determine the fate of the rebellious, subject state. Influenced by the oratory and reasoning of Cleon, one of the most active and eloquent citizens of the time, a majority of the Assembly voted that ALL the male inhabitants of Mytilene should be executed and that the women and children should be sold into slavery – and this, in spite of the fact that many Mytileneans had actively opposed the revolt. A ship was despatched with the order to Paches, the commander on the spot, to comply at once with these decisions.

The Athenians, however, spent a restless and conscience-troubled night. On the following day they formally assembled and passed the resolution of one Diodotus, by which they agreed to execute only those few arrested as responsible for the coup in Mytilene. A second trireme was despatched to countermand the orders carried by the first. Although the first crew had a start of some twenty-four hours, oppressed by the grim mandate which they bore, they rowed without enthusiasm. The second crew ate as they rowed and snatched

[1] *The Peloponnesian War*, trs. Rex Warner (Penguin).

some sleep in turns. They entered the harbour of Mytilene as Paches, having read the first decree, was preparing to act upon it.

The extraordinary case of Mytilene shows the strength and weakness of Athenian democracy. An important point in both debates, as recorded by Thucydides, is that both Cleon and Diodotus appealed only to expediency and purely political considerations. But the expediency of Diodotus was more expedient than that of Cleon.

Twelve years later Athens made an unprovoked attack upon the Aegean island of Melos. The city surrendered. The men of military age were put to death, all other Melians were enslaved and the island was colonised by the Athenians. Here there was no case of revolt. Melos, a colony from Sparta, had not been a member of the Athenian maritime league.

Again Thucydides has recorded what purports to be the debate between the representatives of the two cities. It would be difficult to find in history a more stark and brutal statement of cynical self-interest. 'Our opinion of the gods and our knowledge of men', say the Athenians, 'lead us to conclude that it is a general and necessary law of nature to rule wherever one can. This is not a law that we made ourselves, nor were we the first to act upon it when it was made. We found it already in existence, and we shall leave it to exist for ever among those who come after us.' Eighty-two years earlier the Athenians had sent twenty ships in a fine effort to prevent the city of Miletus from suffering an identical fate at the hands of 'the barbarian'.

What then of the much vaunted Athenian democracy? Was it a sham? Skin deep only? Or was it a solid reality? The answer must be that in spite of certain limitations inherent in the times, the Athenian citizens in the age of Pericles had inherited and evolved an extraordinary degree of democratic control and participation in the running of their state.

Put briefly, the machinery through which this participation was realised was this:

1. Every adult Athenian male was a member of the Assembly which met monthly but could be convened at will – as we saw in the case of Mytilene.
2. To prepare matters for the Assembly there was a Council of 500. This was composed of 50 members of each of the 10 tribes

chosen by ballot. All members were eligible but no man might
serve on the Council more than twice.

3. Each of these groups of 50 acted as a permanent standing com-
   mittee for one tenth part of a year under the guidance of a
   chairman who was chosen from among the members by ballot
   and who, further, presided over the citizen Assembly should it
   be convened.
4. Nine administrative officers, archons, were chosen annually by
   ballot from the number of the Assembly.
5. From the Assembly too were selected, not by ballot, but by
   reputation, ten generals.

It must be stressed that every citizen – there were about 40,000 –
was his own Member of Parliament, in that every citizen was a
member of the Assembly. The size of the state made this possible.
The authority of the Assembly was supreme; all magistrates and
generals could be called to account by it.

Since any Athenian, however slender his means, might find himself archon for a year, or a member of Council, or president of the
Assembly for a day, the citizens considered it right that there should
be a statutory rate of pay for these offices. True, it was not very
great – the idea was that men should undertake these duties as part
of their civic experience and not for remuneration – but it ensured
that the theoretical freedom to hold office was never negated by
financial hardship.

How far Athenian democratic institutions were successful can
perhaps only be known on a fuller acquaintance with the history,
the literature and the visual arts of that state. It has been said, and
with much justification, that it was here in human history that what
men wanted to do and what they had to do most nearly coincided.
There always has been and there always must be some discrepancy
between the ideal men aim at and the reality they produce. In his
famous speech commemorating the Athenian dead in the opening
years of the Peloponnesian War we have a record of Pericles' idea
of his fellow citizens. The discrepancy between the ideal and the
factual was sufficiently small to make Periclean Athens a very remarkable place: to quote one short but characteristic portion of this
funeral oration:

Our love of what is beautiful does not lead to extravagance; our love of things of the mind does not make us soft. We regard wealth as something to be properly used, rather than as something to boast about. As for poverty, no one need be ashamed to admit it: the real shame is in not taking practical measures to escape from it. Here each individual is interested not only in his own affairs but in the affairs of the state as well: even those who are mostly occupied with their own business are extremely well-informed on general politics – this is a peculiarity of ours; we do not say that a man who takes no interest in politics is a man who minds his own business; we say that he has no business here at all. We Athenians, in our own persons, take our decisions on policy or submit them to proper discussions: for we do not think that there is an incompatibility between words and deeds; the worst thing is to rush into action before the consequences have been properly debated. And this is another point where we differ from other people. We are capable at the same time of taking risks and of estimating them beforehand. Others are brave out of ignorance; and, when they stop to think, they begin to fear. But the man who can most truly be accounted brave is he who best knows the meaning of what is sweet in life and of what is terrible, and then goes out undeterred to meet what is to come.[1]

SPARTA

Go, tell at Sparta thou that passest by,
That here, obedient to her word, we lie.

SIMONIDES: *On the Spartan dead at Thermopylae*

The history of Sparta was as stark and strange as its founding was impolitic and inauspicious. Shortly after the Trojan War a body of Dorians invaded the Peloponnese, conquered the inhabitants of Laconia and built their collection of villages, Sparta, on the banks of the river Eurotas. The previous inhabitants of Laconia and the surrounding areas were reduced to slavery (henceforth known as the Helots) so that the Spartans might be free from the menial business of securing a livelihood. Wrapped in a caul of military might and sterile single-mindedness the Spartan community presents as great a contrast to Athens as it is possible to imagine.

The laws and institutions by which Spartan lives were regulated were ascribed to the shadowy figure of Lycurgus. Whether the Spartan constitution is the work of a man called Lycurgus or not,

[1] Ibid., Book II.

indeed whether there was any such historical person at all, is unimportant. Plutarch in his *Life of Lycurgus* has provided us with an eloquent and fascinating account of Spartan life.

According to Plutarch's account, Lycurgus, in preparation for his task, sailed to Egypt, Crete and Asia. In Egypt, 'being much taken with their way of separating the soldiery from the rest of the nation, he transferred it from them to Sparta, a removal from contact with those employed in low and mechanical occupations giving high refinement and beauty to the state'. His reason for visiting Asia after Crete is interesting: 'to examine the difference between the manners and rules of life of the Cretans, which were very sober and temperate, and those of the Ionians, a people of sumptuous and delicate habits, and so to form a judgment; *just as physicians do by comparing healthy and diseased bodies*'.

Lycurgus, fully alive to the evils which overtake a state where extremes of wealth and poverty exist, and determined to expel all arrogance, covetousness, luxury and crime, succeeded in having the land equably divided and in reducing all citizens to an equal footing. If any man wished to be pre-eminent, let him be so in merit and moral worth. This measure was supplemented by the calling in of all silver and gold currency and the substitution of a heavy and wellnigh worthless iron coinage. As a result, hoarding and theft were neatly banished; for, as the originator of the idea drily observed: 'anyone wishing to hoard twenty or thirty pounds will need a large room and anyone wishing to steal it will need nothing less than a yoke of oxen'.

Upon the disappearance of a currency of mobility and value, luxury trades withered – as indeed was intended – and wholesome essentials, such as tables and chairs and drinking cups were much improved.

A final blow was struck against luxury and riches with the ordinance that all should eat in common. Thus none would be tempted to eat reclining on costly couches before splendid tables, enfeebling mind and body by indulgence and excess. None would be tempted to eat better than his neighbour. Their meals were frugal with healthy hunger for their sauce. An Asiatic monarch was said to have imported a Spartan cook to make for him the 'black broth' he had heard so much of. On expressing disappointment he was told by the cook that a swim in the Eurotas was needed to give it relish.

In order that Spartan women should be worthy wives and mothers of Spartan men, girls as well as boys were expected to submit to a strict regime of physical training. Their marriage laws and customs were guided by the dictates of eugenics; family life was to give way to the breeding of well-favoured children. 'And indeed,' writes Plutarch, 'Lycurgus was of a persuasion that children were not so much the property of their parents as of the whole commonwealth. . . .' Infants were inspected by certain elders of the state to see if they were fit for rearing and such as were not, had to be destroyed in a chasm beneath Mt. Taygetus.

Young boys and youths were toughened and accustomed to regular deprivations to a degree which would make our conception of 'Spartan fare' appear in the order of criminal luxury. Initiative and endurance were encouraged through a policy of theft. Boys were to steal to supplement their rations. If caught, they suffered severe whipping, not because the theft was wrong, but because they had been clumsy to a culpable degree. There was the well-known story of the Spartan boy who, having stolen a young fox and having hidden it under his coat, allowed it to tear him to pieces with tooth and claw rather than allow it to be detected. Plutarch, writing about A.D. 100, continues: 'What is practised to this very day in Lacedaemon is enough to gain credit for this story, for I myself have seen several of the youths endure whipping to death at the foot of the altar of Diana.'[1]

Most Greeks from Homeric Odysseus to those Athenians mentioned by St. Paul were immensely robust talkers and captive to the spoken word. Not so the Dorian Spartans. They held the view that just as their short, sharp swords could find the heart of any man, their short, 'Laconic' speech could probe the heart of any matter.

Life for adult Spartans was a kind of prolonged commando training course in a city which bore the aspect of a camp. They enjoyed abundant leisure by virtue of the strictest of Lycurgan injunctions constraining every citizen to 'esteem beneath him the frivolous devotion of time and attention to the mechanical arts and to money-making'. This brings us to the consideration of the Helots without whom this leisure could not have been available, and whose treatment troubled the conscience of many an admirer of the Spartan constitution. The Helots tilled the land and produced all that the

[1] *Life of Lycurgus* (Everyman's Library, Dent).

free-born Spartans needed. But there was, besides, a much more subtle and unsavoury use of Helots. From time to time, as they grew numerous or discontented, the Spartan youth, formed into a kind of secret police force, were despatched to the fields to decimate them as they worked. The state decreed the luckless Helots perpetual outlaws whose death need lie on no man's conscience and whose killing constituted a convenient safety-valve for the over-trained commando youth. More remarkable and more repugnant was the finesse by which the Spartans retained their purity and rectitude while coercing Helots, whom they had first made drunk, to perform unseemly songs and dances and demean themselves.

Lycurgus forbade his citizens to go abroad and banished strangers from his state as far as possible. For concourse with strange peoples would introduce strange words and they in turn would beget unwanted novelty of thought which, like bacteria, would cause a ferment in the state and lead it towards explosion.

What then was the object of Laconian life and to what extent was the object achieved?

By reason of their obedience, bravery and power to endure they were, for generations, peerless fighters, the elite of Greece. As Plutarch remarks: 'If others appeared as the scholars, they appeared as the masters of Greece.' When charged with the task of holding the pass of Thermopylae against the advancing Persians, knowing the odds, they fought to the last man, earning the gratitude of Greece and the moving tribute of Simonides. (When in 371 B.C. the unheard of happened, and the Thebans defeated the Spartans in a pitched battle, a certain philosopher remarked that the victors, in their elation, looked like schoolboys who had beaten their master.) They scorned to wall their city believing that bravery was a greater bulwark than brick.

At home and abroad Spartans had a great reputation for simplicity, modesty, good manners and, on the part of the young, a wholesome respect for their elders. In comparison with the Athenians they were free of interminable wrangles in the law courts. Litigation thrives on property and possessiveness and these the Spartans had forsworn. Communal living was transparent living, unsuited to sedition or personal advancement. Cohesion and rigidity were sought and won – but at a price.

Immune at home from all infections which accompany gold and

encouraged to modesty by corporate life, a Spartan when called abroad on duty was lacking in resistance and proverbially fell. In spite of, or perhaps because of, her strict consideration for eugenics, Sparta's citizen population dwindled rapidly to insignificance. From the traditional date of the introduction of the Lycurgan constitution, no work of art, no building of note, no spark of culture can be ascribed to Sparta. As one contemporary scholar has put it: 'If the Spartans were marked by their "Laconic" speech, that was because they had nothing to say.'[1]

SUGGESTED READING

Any standard history of Greece.
Finley, M. I. *The Ancient Greeks* (Chatto & Windus).
Kitto, H. D. F. *The Greeks* (Pelican).
Plutarch. Lives of Lycurgus and Pericles (Everyman's Library, Dent).

[1] M. I. Finley: *The Greeks* (B.B.C. Publication).

CHAPTER XI

Socrates

Virtue is knowledge.
The unexamined life is not worth living.

SOCRATES

Socrates' life spanned the last seventy years of the fifth century before Christ. He was a young man of thirty when the Parthenon with its sculptures was completed; at the age of forty he would have heard Pericles deliver the funeral oration referred to in the last chapter; one day in his sixty-fourth year it fell to his lot to preside over the citizen Assembly; and in his seventy-first year, having been charged with introducing strange gods to his city and corrupting the minds of the young, he was found guity and condemned to die. The account of his trial and defence, his last discussions with his intimate circle of friends and the closing moments of his life are recorded with brilliance and devotion in Plato's dialogues, *The Apology*, *The Crito* and *The Phaedo*.

What concerns us chiefly here is the claim that Socrates was the pivot on which the course of European thought swung round. What seed did he let fall to be so assiduously caught up and cultivated by Plato?

As a young man, eager to understand the world, he studied the theories of Anaximenes, Empedocles and Anaxagoras and the other natural philosophers. For Socrates these systems all lacked, purpose and design. We can catch a glimpse of what he was seeking when he says he turned from his contemporary Anaxagoras in disgust and disappointment when that philosopher introduced Mind only to set his world in motion, thereafter leaving it to be cared for by a sightless and soulless natural law. In short, to explain what the world *was made of* – whether in terms of unity or no – and to explain its movement, was no explanation at all. Why, you might as well try to give an adequate 'explanation' of the phenomenon, Socrates, by cataloguing the sinews, muscles, bones and tendons of which he was composed and you might as well try to 'explain' his movements through the Attic countryside by saying that these sinews and muscles contracted and relaxed. That, argued Socrates, was an inadequate explanation of the full significance of him or anyone else. As a philosophic 'cause' it fell far short of what he would consider satisfactory.

But there was another kind of knowledge which Socrates felt compelled to pursue: the knowledge of Truth, Justice, Goodness. For how could any man know how to live wisely as a member of a community – let alone an empire – unless a knowledge of these was possible? The trouble was that no one seemed to have a single conception of these things. What had been 'bad' for Miletus before the Persian war was 'good' for Melos in later years. What democratic Athens thought of as 'just' would seem the negation of 'justice' to the Spartan oligarchy. Indeed it was worse than that: had not in the case of Mytilene the most responsible citizens of Athens voted differently on two successive days as to what was 'good' for their city? This would indicate that they did not even vote according to self-interest – for how could their interests have changed over night?

The problem was both aggravated and made more urgent in Socrates' lifetime in that a class of professional teachers had emerged in Athens and other cities who – for a fee – taught young men to be skilled in oratory and disputation and how, if necessary, to make the false seem true and the better cause appear the worse – a valuable asset in a litigious state. Socrates in his quest for knowledge abominated these Sophists – as they were called – with their magpie minds and facile lip-service to wisdom.

Socrates, who lived most frugally, was not obliged to work in order to earn a living. He spent most of his time, indoors or out, talking, listening and thinking. His custom of observing the artisans of Athens at their work and using them to illustrate his arguments became a joke amongst his friends. But it led to one of the cardinal elements in his teaching: if the shoemaker is the right man to make a pair of shoes, if the carpenter is the right man to make a chair, a wine grower the right man to give a judgment on a wine, who is equipped to speak of Justice, Truth, Statecraft and such vital matters?

It came as no small surprise to Socrates while engaged on this pursuit to learn that the Oracle at Delphi pronounced him to be the wisest man in Greece. After all, he could not even make a pair of shoes much less define the Good, the Beautiful and the True. What mystified him more was that politicians, philosophers and poets who claimed to understand these things were found in reality to be ignorant of them when put to the test. He found too that no one appeared to be able to probe beneath the surface of life to discover the reality which – he felt sure – was there. If asked what essential virtue was, people tended to tell him about manly virtue, a woman's virtue, a child's virtue, a slave's virtue, but never about Virtue itself.

Socrates, therefore, concluded that the only sense in which he could be considered wiser than others was that all men lacked knowledge of the greatest things in life but he alone was aware of this ignorance and, consequently, in a position to remedy it. So if evil in this life arose from ignorance, Virtue must be equated with knowledge. Men act foolishly, perversely and wickedly because they do not KNOW what is best for them.

Not everyone would agree that good living was contingent merely on perception of the Good. The pagan poet Ovid wrote: 'Video meliora proboque, deteriora sequor,'[1] and St. Paul said with some feeling: 'The good that I would I do not, and the evil which I would not, that I do.' But Socrates was endowed with unusual powers of will and endurance. On active service in northern regions he had performed prodigies of physical endurance, stalking over ice bare-footed and scantily clad more easily than did his fellow soldiers in their boots. Men wondered at his ability to carouse without showing the least signs of drunkenness. He would stand for hours in abstracted concentration in an effort to solve some problem which had gripped him. In battle he was cool and fearless.

But if the good life depended on knowledge of the essence of The Good, how was this knowledge to be obtained? Firstly, by means of the mental exercise of the dialectic which was admirably suited to the Socratic method of investigation. The word is from the Greek verb *dialegesthai* meaning 'to have a discussion with someone' – and what could have suited Socrates better? But in his hands it came to be an exacting process of question and answer in the course of which all non-essential layers of husk were peeled off and the final grain of truth revealed. It was a process which incurred some unpopularity for its formidable exponent. Even his good friend Meno protested

[1] 'I see the better course and approve of it, but I follow the worse.'

that under interrogation Socrates benumbed him like the electric-ray (torpedo fish), and at his trial Socrates claimed that he had plagued his fellow citizens like a gad-fly sent by God to keep them morally alert and 'if in your annoyance you finish me off with a single slap, you will go on sleeping till the end of your days, unless God in his care sends someone to take my place'.[1]

The second approach to knowledge lay partly in this world and partly in the next. 'Either', argues Socrates before his judges, 'death is annihilation, and the dead have no consciousness of anything; or, as we are told, it is really a change: a migration of the soul from this place to another.'[2] Now Socrates' entire manner of living and more particularly the manner of his death were based on the conviction that the second alternative was the truth. He believed that after death he would arrive in the land of his heart's desire 'to parley with the pure, oracular dead' – a privilege for which he asserts he is prepared to die ten times over. But there was a vital condition upon which this translation after death depended, a condition which not many Athenians of the time would have been prepared to accept. This was that thoughts of all material pleasures and comfort should give way to the 'tendance of the soul', that in living, men should practise dying. As Pythagoras foreshadowed the abbot leading his brother-hood, so Socrates – who was nothing if not consistent – was the forerunner of the dedicated friar.

This brings us closer to an understanding of the grounds on which Socrates criticised his native state, advanced democracy though it was. The more a state was democratic the more the administration was in the hands of amateurs. The fullers, the joiners, the weavers, the blacksmiths and the potters were excellent fellows in their own way; but the more devoted they were to their respective trades, the less could they train the soul to apprehend those requisites for state-craft: Justice, Goodness and Truth. On the other hand, the rich could hardly be expected any more than the artisans to practise the pursuit of these absolutes. They could not afford to neglect their finances, their real estate, their law-suits and their luxuries. It permanently outraged and genuinely appalled Socrates that men should entrust the ship of state to pilots who had never learned the barest rudiments of navigation, who had never raised their eyes for long enough to learn the difference between a drachma and a star.

[1] Plato: *Apology*, trs. Hugh Tredennick (Penguin).   [2] Ibid.

Why, the day he had presided over the Assembly the whole citizen body, choked like children by emotion and heedless of the city's laws, were clamouring for the summary execution of all the generals who had failed to rescue sailors overboard after the naval victory at Arginusae! Had he not faced them as fearlessly as he did their enemies, another miscarriage of justice would have been laid at democracy's door.

Socrates, in short, did not believe that τὸ καλόν (the Beautiful) could be decreed in the market place teeming, as it was, not only with men who were pulled this way and that by self-interest, but who, in the pursuits of such abstracts, were amateurs and proud of it.

In a city renowned for drama Socrates acquired a habit of making exits – dramatic and alone. After the famous banquet at the house of Agathon, the tragic poet, when by dawn Socrates had drunk and talked the other guests to slumber, he went home. After the unseemly affair of Arginusae, he quit the Assembly and went home. On the famous occasion when ordered by the thirty tyrants – who had temporarily supplanted the democracy – unlawfully to arrest an innocent fellow citizen, he simply went home. And finally when Athens could tolerate the goading of the gad-fly no longer, Socrates, composed and confident, drank the appointed potion and 'went home'. Whether that is merely a euphemism or whether his soul went on to try a fall in dialectic with Ajax and Odysseus was the burden of his life's teaching and much of Plato's writing. We can imagine the Athenians murmuring with Aristophanes: 'A plague to us, he'll plague them all in Hell.'

CHAPTER XII

Plato (1). The Theory

Plato thought nature but a spume that plays
Upon a ghostly paradigm of things.

W. B. YEATS

When Aristotle from the barbarous north arrived in Athens he found a flourishing centre of learning and philosophy founded by Plato in the shady grove of Academus. The 'Academy', as it was called – the first of Europe's universities – was opened in 387 B.C. and after a period of nine hundred years was closed by the Emperor Justinian. Within these shady precincts young men met to undergo a rigorous discipline in mathematics, music and astronomy. The Academy was not merely a secular institution. It had been conceived of and registered by its founder as a temple of the Muses and like most temples its portals were surmounted by an inscription. It read: 'Let no one who is ignorant of geometry enter here.' Aristotle – presumably proficient in geometry – enrolled and studied there until he left to strike out independently with a centre of his own in the grove of Lycean Apollo. That the Academy and Lyceum (*Lycée*), while predominantly associated with serious education still, should be connected with entertainment – however tenuously – would shock both men profoundly.

It must surely strike a modern reader as odd that the first Academy should have professed some holy obligation and that its fulfilment should be dependent on geometry. Although we have no record of the content of the lectures, we have abundant evidence of Plato's purpose and procedure from his published works. These number some twenty-seven dialogues two of which – *The Republic* and *The Laws* – are long. In all but a few, Socrates is the central character and the philosophical ideas are developed through him.

We can see the scheme of Plato absorbing the elements of his predecessors, shaped to some extent by the historical Socrates and 'fused in the emotive furnace' of the dreadful war. Of all these earlier philosophers Pythagoras is nearest to Plato in spirit, and from this source Plato drew most deeply. Parmenides and Zeno stand revered by Plato – perhaps with an increasing significance in later life – for it was chiefly they who taught the unreality of the palpable world and the worthlessness of man's perception of it by the senses. Although between Plato and the Ionians a great spiritual gulf was fixed, Heraclitus' preoccupation with the mutability of matter and the flux of time was ever present in the Dialogues.

Central in Plato's thought is the theory of Ideas or Forms, from which the name and concept of philosophical Idealism are derived. Plato, like Socrates, was convinced that much of the shallowness of men lay in the fact that they were content to accept appearance for reality, in their inability to distinguish between a worthless fragment of an object and the thing itself. No man can tell whether his individual, isolated acts are good until he has defined the Good. It is dangerously near-sighted to say that the laws have treated a particular person on a particular occasion justly or unjustly, unless one has first attempted a universal definition of Justice. Who could claim any serious understanding of men, or horses, or tables or chairs from a superficial acquaintance with only a number of each? Furthermore, thought Plato, there must be some good reason for each thing having the form it has and no other. It is not enough to say that a man is an assembly of atoms and that a chair is something assembled by a carpenter.

Plato's conclusion was that somewhere there must exist the true, original and essential Forms, of which terrestrial objects were but pale, ephemeral and imperfect reflections. He wanted to get away from the common mistake of confusing poor fragmented specimens of a concept with the whole concept itself in the way that a child might identify a bagful of greasy copper coins with wealth.

In connection with this doctrine, confusion can easily arise through the use of the words 'Idea' and 'Ideal', the usual meaning of which is a private notion in the mind. For Plato these essences have a separate world, the world of Ideas, where they exist unchanging and eternal. Not only are the Ideas of concrete objects to be found there, but even more important, the Ideas of those abstracts – knowledge of which is indispensable for men – the Just, the True, the Beautiful and the Good. To say that these Ideas or Forms are real would be a serious understatement: it is *only* they that are truly real. A man is only man because he 'participates in' the Idea of man, the Ideal horse has imparted form unto the terrestrial horse to make it what it is.

From time to time in Plato's close-knit arguments a point was reached where a leap of faith on the part of the reader or listener was required to gain the summit. At this point, partly to strengthen the faith of the faltering, partly perhaps to distract the attention of the tremulous from the lack of solid ground beneath and partly to display the metaphysical in familiar terms, Plato had a poetic way of breaking into myth. In the seventh book of *The Republic*, allegedly to assist those whose intellectual powers may have difficulty in grasping his theory of Ideas, Plato restores the confidence of the weakest by the simple, familiar imagery of the dwellers in the cave.

Imagine, said Plato, a cave inhabited by creatures who have never seen the outside world of comparative light and liberty. These prisoners are shackled in the deep recess of the cave facing the innermost wall. Behind them is an elevated parapet along which objects pass and whose shadows are projected on the wall by a great fire placed between them and the entrance to the cave. These unfortunate creatures, limited in vision, restricted in movement, dark in understanding, mistake the mural shadow-play for solid things.

Suppose then, continues Plato, that one of those prisoners could be led to the sunlight outside the cave. Imagine the contrast, imagine the amazement in his soul, the wonder that would accompany the exchange of such a shadow for such a substance. Suppose too that this prisoner whose soul has been flooded with light should return to his fellow prisoners in the cave and attempt to drag them up the stony, steep ascent. Would they not resist him as a madman and even kill him?

Such was Plato's allegorical account of his theory of Ideas and, incidentally, of the fate of Socrates.

How, though, in real life can one have cognisance of the world of Forms? What for us is the equivalent of the prisoner's exit from the cave? We have already seen the answer to this in discussing the Orphics and Pythagoras. We have immortal souls which had their origin in that same world and which knew the abiding Forms of things before their incarnation and which will return to them again – provided they have practised the upward-striving discipline of philosophy during life. This is the explanation of the other-worldliness of Socrates; this is what Socrates meant by saying that the soul must always 'practise dying'; this is the significance of Socrates' last words on earth, spoken as the drowsy hemlock benumbed his senses: 'Crito, we ought to offer a cock to Asclepius. See to it and don't forget.' Asclepius the God of healing is to receive a thank-offering in anticipation of the sufferer awakening restored 'after life's fitful fever'.

But what if the soul is not immortal? What of the Atomists and other Ionian materialist views? What if there were no gods, or at any rate no gods who concerned themselves with the creatures of this earth? In Plato's scheme of things the immortal soul is the link between this illusory world and that of the enduring reality of the Forms. Without this, the Forms, although they might exist, would be unknowable. It is little wonder then that the dialogue devoted to the arguments in favour of the soul's immortality, *The Phaedo*, should be amongst the outstanding and most persuasive of Plato's works. *The Phaedo* has the added dramatic weight of recording Socrates' last day on earth in which he defends his whole way of life and comforts those he is about to leave. The argument is sustained and cogent, the writing is gentle and wonderfully humane. In the end, however, we realise there is no final proof – for if there were, metaphysics would cease to be metaphysics – and one of the circle says: 'All the same, the subject is so vast, and I have such a poor opinion of our weak human nature, that I can't help feeling still some misgivings.' At this point Socrates embarks upon a myth similar in essence to the allegory of the cave and at the end explains: 'We should use such accounts to inspire ourselves with confidence, that is why I have already drawn out my tale so long.'

Assuming then the existence of the world of Forms, the immortality of the soul and its origin in that world, what indication is there that the soul retains any memory of the Forms once it has become incarnate? Plato held that the soul at birth forgot its knowledge of the Good, the Beautiful and the other absolutes but that under suitable education and evocation those memories could come seeping through to consciousness. This process Plato called Anamnesis, which simply means 'remembering'. It was precisely this the poet Wordsworth had in mind when he wrote:

Our birth is but a sleep and a forgetting;
The Soul that rises with us, our life's Star,
Hath had elsewhere its setting,
And cometh from afar.[1]

There is an interesting demonstration of the process of Anamnesis at work in the dialogue called after Socrates' friend Meno, a dialogue written by Plato during the period in which he was working out his theory of Ideas. The dialogue opens with Meno asking Socrates: 'Can you tell me Socrates – is virtue something that can be taught? Or does it come by practice? Or is it neither teaching nor practice that gives it to a man but natural aptitude or something else?'

In the course of his reply, loaded with banter and the irony for which he was noted, Socrates says: 'At any rate if you put your question to any of our people, they will all alike laugh and say: "You must think I am singularly fortunate, to know whether virtue can be taught or how it is acquired. The fact is that far from knowing whether it can be taught, I have no idea what virtue itself is. That is my own case. I share the poverty of my fellow-countrymen in this respect, and confess to my shame that I have no knowledge of virtue at all. And how can I know a property of something when I don't even know what it is?" '[2]

As the argument develops, Socrates says: 'Thus the soul, since it is immortal and has been born many times, and has seen all things both here and in the other world, has learned everything that is. So we need not be surprised if it can recall the knowledge of virtue or anything else which, as we can see, it once possessed . . . for seeking and learning are in fact NOTHING BUT RECOLLECTION.'[3]

This is then put to the test. One of Meno's slave-boys is called in. Socrates draws a square on the sand and asks the boy if it is possbile to construct another square double the area of the given one. The boy – who would, of course, have had no contact whatsoever with formal education – agrees that it can be done. Then by a process of question and answer, with Socrates constructing the necessary figures on the sand, they arrive together at the conclusion that the square on the diagonal of the original square is double its area. The boy has originated nothing, on the other hand Socrates has told him

[1] *Ode on Intimations of Immortality.*
[2] *The Meno*, trs. W. K. C. Guthrie, p. 115 (Penguin).
[3] Ibid., pp. 129-30.

nothing. All he claims to have done is to have assisted the boy to become aware of knowledge which he had possessed from the start.

Clearly then if the soul possessed true knowledge during its life in the other world and the ills of this world resulted from its descent into body, whatever could reawaken the recollection of that knowledge was of the utmost importance. Hence it was that Plato insisted on geometry for his initiates and hence it was that foremost among his educational measures he treasured the Dialectic. Zeno was said to have been the first to employ the dialectic method; Socrates subjected members of his Athenian audience to it continually and Plato insisted on it as the wing on which the soul momentarily soared above the miasma of our earth's clogging atmosphere to catch a fleeting glimpse of Truth. In this way knowledge was attained by a purely intellectual and intuitive process independently of sense, perception and experience.

But so important in his scheme of things is Plato's theory of knowledge and so intimately is it associated with his theory of Forms, that more must be said about it. We find the essence of the theory stated quite clearly in the dialogue *The Phaedo*:

SOCRATES Now take the acquisition of knowledge; is the body a hindrance or not, if one takes it into partnership to share an investigation? What I mean is this: is there any certainty in human sight and hearing, or is it true, as the poets are always dinning into our ears, that we neither hear nor see anything accurately? Yet if these senses are not clear and accurate, the rest can hardly be so, because they are all inferior to the first two. Don't you agree?

SIMMIAS Certainly.

SOCRATES Then when is it that the soul attains to truth? When it tries to investigate anything with the help of the body, it is obviously led astray.

SIMMIAS Quite so.

SOCRATES Is it not in the course of reflection, if at all, that the soul gets a clear view of facts?

SIMMIAS Yes.

SOCRATES Surely the soul can best reflect when it is free of all distractions such as hearing or sight or pain or pleasure of any kind – that is, when it ignores the body and becomes as far as possible independent, avoiding all

physical contacts and associations as much as it can, in
its search for reality.

SIMMIAS   That is so.

SOCRATES Then here too – in despising the body and avoiding it,
and endeavouring to become independent – the
philosopher's soul is ahead of all the rest.

SIMMIAS   It seems so.

SOCRATES Here are some more questions, Simmias. Do we recognise such a thing as absolute uprightness?

SIMMIAS   Indeed we do.

SOCRATES And absolute beauty and goodness too?

SIMMIAS   Of course.

SOCRATES Have you ever seen any of these things with your eyes?

SIMMIAS   Certainly not.

SOCRATES Well, have you ever apprehended them with any other
bodily sense? By 'them' I mean not only absolute
tallness or health or strength, but the real nature of any
given thing – what it actually is. Is it through the body
that we get the truest perception of them? Isn't it true
that in any enquiry you are likely to attain more
nearly to knowledge of your object in proportion to
the care and accuracy with which you have prepared
yourself to understand that object in itself?

SIMMIAS   Certainly.

SOCRATES Don't you think that the person who is likely to succeed
in this attempt most perfectly is the one who approaches
each object, as far as possible, with the unaided intellect, without taking account of any sense of sight in
his thinking, or dragging any other sense into his
reckoning – the man who pursues the truth by applying
his pure and unadulterated thought to the pure and
unadulterated object, cutting himself off as much as
possible from his eyes and ears and virtually all the
rest of his body, as an impediment which by its presence
prevents the soul from attaining to truth and clear
thinking? Is not this the person, Simmias, who will
reach the goal of reality, if anybody can?

SIMMIAS   What you say is absolutely true, Socrates.[1]

And again, later in the same dialogue:

[1] *The Phaedo*: trs. Hugh Tredennick, pp. 83-5 of *The Last Days of Socrates*
(Penguin).

SOCRATES Did we not say some time ago that when the soul uses the instrumentality of the body for any enquiry, whether through sight or hearing or any other sense (because using the body implies using the senses) it is drawn away by the body into the realm of the variable, and loses its way and becomes confused and dizzy, as though it were fuddled, through contact with things of a similar nature?

CEBES Certainly.

SOCRATES But when it investigates by itself, it passes into the realm of the pure and everlasting and immortal and changeless; and being of a kindred nature, when it is once independent and free from interference, consorts with it always and strays no longer, but remains, in that realm of the absolute, constant and invariable, through contact with beings of a similar nature. And this condition of the soul we call Wisdom.[1]

Here we have a very clear statement of the doctrine that knowledge and the manifold variables in the shape of particular objects of this world have nothing in common. The poet, Ezra Pound, once wrote when addressing absolute Beauty:

> Even in my dreams you have denied yourself to me
> And sent me only your handmaids.

In Plato's scheme of things as stated, experiences gained through the senses cannot even play the part of 'handmaids' to knowledge; they merely confuse and befuddle.

In a very much later dialogue, *The Theaetetus*, Plato returned to a more specific treatment of the problem of defining knowledge. Quite apart from the obvious necessity of providing a consistent theory of epistemology, Plato was compelled to publish an answer to the highly subjective and unashamedly utilitarian teaching of the Sophists, the men who loved, in public, as the late Louis MacNeice once wrote,

> To draw the cork out of an old conundrum
> And watch the paradoxes fizz.

The Sophists were not only a symptom of the civic malaise which Plato felt called upon to remedy, they themselves were part of it.

[1] Ibid., p. 105.

If they were prepared for a fee – as they were – on one day to teach the new and comparatively affluent generation that a given thing X is white or good, and on the following day that X is black or bad, this was flux with a vengeance. No doubt there was a very great deal of cheap and shallow disputation in Athens and the Greek world during the early years of Plato's life. Much of it became fashionable by the demand on the part of young men for higher education coupled with the severely practical need of men in an increasingly property-conscious and increasingly litigious community to be capable of defending themselves in the city law-courts. A well-known example of this smart, less creditable application of knowledge was the sophist who claimed *à propos* Heracleitus' theory of flux, 'It's no use claiming today payment of a debt contracted by my client last month; he is not the man he was last month!'

There were, however, Sophists who stood head and shoulders above the common run of their fellows. Such a one was Protagoras. He hailed from Abdera, the birthplace of Democritus, and lived and lectured in Athens from the high days of Pericles until about 415 B.C. If we are to judge from Plato's description of the views of Protagoras, embodied in a most interesting dialogue of the same name, not only was he a teacher of great repute and integrity, but he preserved and fostered the finest elements in the Ionian tradition of thought and speculation. The kernel of Protagoras' philosophy is contained in his famous dictum: 'Man is the measure of all things, of those that are that they are, and of those that are not that they are not.'

Such a doctrine, of course, robbed both virtue and knowledge of any possibility of those absolute and stable qualities which Plato so earnestly sought and reduced them each to a kind of mirage, the product of disordered senses, subject to the deceptive play of light and shade, altered from moment to moment by man and circumstance. The teaching of Protagoras might indeed be on a loftier plane than that of the average Sophist, but it was, from the point of view of content and attitude, as highly subjective and as dangerously relative as theirs. One might say with truth that the whole of Plato's life was devoted to the refutation of such relativist theories. But in two dialogues, *The Protagoras* and *The Theaetetus*, the one early and the other comparatively late in the order of his writings, Plato dealt with this problem specifically and anchored both Virtue and Knowledge securely to the abiding bed-rock of the absolute.

Turning for a moment to *The Theaetetus* (reference to the significance of *The Protagoras* will be found in the next chapter) we find that although the main argument moves towards the same end as that outlined in the quotations from the Phaedo above, two points emerge as being worthy of comment. The first is that Plato in the later dialogue is somewhat less dogmatic and less positive about what knowledge is and where it lies. He tells us rather what it is not:

SOCRATES   Therefore, Theaetetus, neither perception nor true belief, nor an account coupled with true belief can be knowledge.
THEAETETUS   I suppose not.

The second point is that one cannot but be impressed by the importance attributed in this dialogue to experience. Although knowledge still resides with and emanates from God and the world of Forms, anamnesis has quietly yielded place to experience. To take only one of many possible examples:

SOCRATES   Good heavens, boy! have you never heard that I am the son of a fine buxom midwife called Phainarete?
THEAETETUS   Yes, I have heard as much.
SOCRATES   And have you also heard that I also practise the same art?
THEAETETUS   No, never.
SOCRATES   Well I do; but be sure not to tell the others. It is not known that I possess this skill; so the ignorant describe me in other terms as an eccentric who drives men to distraction. Have you heard that too?
THEAETETUS   I have indeed.
SOCRATES   Shall I tell you the reason?
THEAETETUS   Please do.
SOCRATES   Consider the general practice of midwives and you will understand more clearly what I mean. You are doubtless aware that none of them ever attends other women in childbirth so long as she herself is capable of conceiving and bearing children, but only when she is too old to do so.
THEAETETUS   Of course.
SOCRATES   They say that is because Artemis, the patroness of childbirth is herself childless. She would not allow barren women to act as midwives, because it is beyond the power of human nature to acquire skill

without experience; and she therefore assigned the duty to women who were past childbearing, as a mark of respect for their resemblance to herself.[1]

Although there is in this dialogue a considerable modification of the standpoint adopted in *The Phaedo*, it is still made clear that Protagoras represents a heresy and that the teaching of the mainstream of the Ionian thinkers about the acquisition and nature of knowledge is not to be tolerated.

There is in dialogues such as *The Theaetetus* a certain amount of vivid and vigorous antipathy towards many of the pre-Socratic thinkers. Nevertheless, it is interesting to note to what a large extent Plato, in these later dialogues, acted as a watershed for these preceding streams of thought. Nowhere is this more fascinatingly apparent than in that strange account of the creation of our world and ordering of our cosmos – *The Timaeus*. Plato's predecessors, as we have come to know them, were primarily concerned with questions of 'how? and from what origin?' and with speculations in physics and cosmogony. Plato was preoccupied with the question 'why? and to what end?' and with the formulation of a system of ethics. In *The Timaeus* we find a physical and speculative account of the creation worked out in terms of the Platonic theory of Forms and knowledge.

Stated briefly the scheme is this. The All-Creator (who may be identified with a good God or the principle of Reason) and the Forms are uncreated, unchanging and real, while this earth, which the Creator has caused to be made, is always in a state of becoming and so can never be real, can never be the object of true knowledge. The Creator is good; Reason permeates all; and the world is fashioned in imitation of the eternal Forms. All things which have been created have been so for the best and in the best possible way. The world cannot be the resultant of blind, fortuitous movement as, for example, Heracleitus and the atomists had held. Soul existed prior to body and was ordained to be the 'body's mistress and governor'.

For Plato, therefore, creation involved a static universe where all things were arranged for the best in the best of all possible worlds. Development and evolutionary process were ruled out. For example:

. . . and the gods, holding that the front is more honourable and

[1] *The Theaitetos*, trs. John Warrington, p. 75 of *Parmenides and Other Dialogues* (Everyman's Library, Dent).

fit to lead than the back, gave us movement for the most part in that direction. So man must needs have the front of the body distinguished and unlike the back; so first they set the face on the globe of the head on that side and fixed in it organs for all the forethought of the soul, and appointed this, our natural front, to be the part having leadership.[1]

Teeth, tongue and lips were fashioned, just as we know them, so that man might eat and speak. The universe was flooded with light so that eyes might see. Rain fell that crops might grow. The earth produced crops that man might be nourished. It was this doctrine that all things in the universe were ordained by Reason for an appointed end or goal which earned for Plato the distinction of being Europe's first great teleological thinker.

It is not wholly true to say that creation in *The Timaeus* was static. Since Reason created all, and for the best, there could be no improvement. There could be, however, and indeed there was, movement in a downward direction, a kind of punitive downgrading. For example, 'harmless but lightwitted men, who studied the heavens but imagined in their simplicity that the surest evidence in these matters comes through the eye', might grow feathers and be transformed into birds. Again: 'Land animals came from men who had no use for philosophy . . . and, finally, men who were most foolish and stupid of all might be transformed into fish and all that live in the water.'[2] Here again we see how Plato and the tentatively evolutionary thinkers such as Anaximander, Empedocles and Protagoras, were not merely in disagreement but in fundamental opposition. Empedocles had envisaged nature as a kind of life-force producing all kinds of creatures – beautiful or grotesque – by a system of trial and error; Anaximander held that man might have come from fish while Plato held that fish might be fallen man.

One of the most interesting theories in this work is that which embodies Plato's contribution to the great debate on the structure of matter. Here Plato accepts the thesis of Empedocles that matter consists of four elements: Fire, Air, Water and Earth. Then, having regard to the nature of the world and the creation he has earlier postulated he poses the question: If there are four primary elements, what are the most perfect shapes that can be constructed, unlike each

[1] *The Timaeus*, trs. F. M. Cornford, p. 151 (Routledge).
[2] Ibid., p. 358.

other, but such that they can be resolved each into the other as are the elements from time to time? For answer Plato harks back to Pythagoras and assigns to each of the four elements the shape of one of the five regular solids: to fire, the regular tetrahedron; to air, the regular octahedron; to water the regular icosahedron; to earth the cube.

| Fire | Air | Water | Earth | Cosmos |

At this point comes a surprise. Plato for all his hostility towards Democritus, for all his philosophical divergence from the atomists, adopts an atomic programme. Not only are the shapes of these regular solids 'the best', but three of them, i.e. all save the cube, have something in common. All have equilateral triangular faces each of which can be further divided into two right-angled triangles having sides 1, 2, $\sqrt{3}$. Now where Democritus postulated atoms of different shapes combining and recombining to produce manifold and differing substances, Plato postulated right-angled triangles with sides 1, 2, $\sqrt{3}$, capable of interchange between elements of fire, air and water. Earth, being represented by the cube and therefore having faces composed of two right-angled triangles having sides 1, 1, $\sqrt{2}$, was not capable of interchange with the other elements. So where Pythagoras constructed matter with discrete points, where the Eleatics insisted on a continuum, where Democritus envisaged atoms of an infinite number of irregular shapes, Plato posited two orderly, disciplined right-angled triangles, one having sides 1, 2, $\sqrt{3}$, the other having sides 1, 1, $\sqrt{2}$. He then states in the accredited atomist way: 'Now we must think of all these bodies as so small that a single body of any one of these kinds is invisible to us because of its smallness; though when a number are aggregated the masses of them can be seen.'

There is, however, more to be said about these triangles. Professor Popper – one of the most stimulating of modern writers on Greek Philosophy – has advanced the theory that the discovery of the irrationality of the square root of two may not have been known to Democritus (the date of the discovery is in some doubt) and that this discovery was as fatal a blow to atomism as it was to Pythagoreanism. Professor Popper writes:

> Both theories were based on the doctrine that all measurement is, ultimately, counting of natural units, so that every measurement must be reducible to pure numbers. The distance between any two atomic points must, therefore, consist of a number of atomic distances; thus all distances must be commensurable. But this turns out to be impossible even in the simple case of the distances between the corners of a square, because of the incommensurability of the diagonal *d* with the side *a*.[1]

So we are faced with an even more unexpected sight than that of Plato adopting an atomic theory – that of Plato saving the Democritean atomic theory. By incorporating the irrationals in the structure of matter in a geometrical rather than an arithmetical way, he had neutralised their destructive power; he had made them safe.

But Plato's triangles are only two-dimensional triangles. If we do not assign thickness to them, they will not add up to solids. If we do assign thickness to them, it will have to be an atomic thickness and we find that the difficulty which had been eliminated in one plane has returned in another. As the ancient Chinese philosopher said in considering the same triangles: 'That which has no thickness cannot be piled up, but it can cover a thousand square miles in area.'

The Platonic regular solids have always provided interest for mathematicians; there is a certain fascination in the numerical relationship of apex, face and edge. Their importance is being discussed anew now that virologists have discovered that certain virus particles appear to be regular icosahedra. There is undeniably something exciting in seeing those triangular faces which Plato and his contemporary mathematicians assigned to the smallest particles of nature being brought into view by a modern electron microscope. One must bear in mind, however, that Plato almost certainly received the idea from Pythagoras who in turn received it from nature's crystals on his father's bench, and that as far as we can tell from his published works, Plato would not have approved of our attempts to approach knowledge and truth through the medium of the electron microscope.

Some commentators assume *The Timaeus* to be no more than a

[1] Karl R. Popper, *Conjectures and Refutations*, p. 83 (Routledge).

mythical account of man and his environment. If it is not a scientific account of the origin of man, it is, at any rate, an account of those things descriptions of which we normally look to science to provide. Such an account of things which yield their secrets more readily to the empiricist and close observationist, when written, as here, from a thoroughgoing a-priorist and metaphysical point of view, tends to be an amalgam of the brilliant and the grotesque. The dichotomy between body and soul, this-worldliness and other-worldliness, is widened and deepened. For Timaeus, who was a Pythagorean, and for Plato, the 'slumbrous mass', the matter of this world, was created by the triangle. In Egypt, a country which greatly influenced both Pythagoras and Plato, it was the Nile's amorphous mud – the symbol of creation for those who knew it – which created the form of the triangle.

SUGGESTED READING

The following Dialogues of Plato are available in Penguin Classics:
The Last Days of Socrates (contains *The Apology, The Crito and The Phaedo*),
    Gorgias, Protagoras and Meno, The Republic, Symposium.

CHAPTER XIII

Plato (2). The Republic

Civilisation is hooped together, brought
Under a rule, under the semblance of peace
By manifold illusion.

W. B. YEATS

Plato's Republic was a reply to a thesis which was current both in everyday life and in certain writings in Athens during the latter half of the fifth century B.C. The thesis was that, whereas only a person who had acquired skills could make such things as shoes and ships, all men could have a sense of justice and civic duty.

To take the practical application first. 'We do not say', declared Pericles in the funeral oration, 'that a man who takes no interest in politics is a man who minds his own business, we say he has no business here at all.' Not only was it possible for every adult male Athenian to accept direct responsibility for government, it was expected of him. The size and political structure of this city-state made every citizen, as it were, his own Member of Parliament. Since every man was liable to soldier with his fellow citizens, help to man or equip a warship, take his seat on the panel of judges in courts of law and speak in or even preside over the Assembly, no mystique of government, no 'secluded corridors of power' had yet arisen. There was no one so influential or so exalted but felt every puff of popular breath that blew from the Assembly on the hill called Pnyx.

One of the chief philosophical exponents of the thesis was Protagoras. Since, unfortunately, a work which he wrote on the foundations of society has perished, we must use the words attributed to him by Plato in the dialogue *Protagoras*.

Protagoras is telling Socrates how the gods had charged Prometheus and Epimetheus with the task of equipping the emergent creatures of the earth with suitable powers. He continues:

Now Epimetheus begged Prometheus to allow him to do the

distribution himself – 'and when I have done it' he said, 'you can review it'. So he persuaded him and set to work. In his allotment he gave to some creatures strength without speed, and equipped the weaker kinds with speed. Some he armed with weapons, while to the unarmed he gave some other faculty and so contrived means for their preservation. To those that he endowed with smallness, he granted winged flight or a dwelling underground; to those which he increased in stature, their size itself was a protection. Thus he made his whole distribution on a principle of compensation, being careful by these devices that no species should be destroyed. . . . Prometheus came to inspect the work, and found the other animals well off for everything, but man naked, unshod, unbedded and unarmed: and already the appointed day had come, when man too was to emerge from within the earth into the daylight. Prometheus therefore, being at a loss to provide any means of salvation for man, stole from Hephaestus and Athena the gift of skill in the arts, together with fire – for without fire it was impossible for anyone to possess or use this skill – and bestowed it on man. In this way man acquired sufficient resources to keep himself alive, but had no political wisdom. This was in the keeping of Zeus. . . . Zeus therefore, fearing the total destruction of our race, sent Hermes to impart to men the qualities of respect for others and a sense of justice, so as to bring order into our cities and create a bond of friendship and union. Hermes asked Zeus in what manner he was to bestow these gifts on men. 'Shall I distribute them as the arts were distributed – that is, on the principle that one trained doctor suffices for many laymen, and so with the other experts? Shall I distribute justice and respect for their fellows in this way, or to all alike?' 'TO ALL' said Zeus. 'LET ALL HAVE THEIR SHARE. . . .'[1]

Such a theme ran directly counter to all that Plato believed. He felt that the staves of the cask of civilisation were falling apart; that the hoop was slipping; that he must prove himself to be society's master cooper.

The Republic opens with the search for a definition of justice and ends with an Orphic myth in which we are assured of justice in the life hereafter. Thrasymachus, typical of the non-philosophic, the non-defining man, asserts with force that justice is nothing more than the interest of the stronger party; in all states justice is the interest of the established government. He points out that when a

_____
[1] *Protagoras*, pp. 52ff (Penguin).

little man is discovered in an act of injustice he is branded as a burglar, swindler, thief and brigand. If, however, the same acts are committed on a large scale by a government or a prince or a tyrant, they will be hailed as the consummation of justice and attract honour and flattery for the instigator.

The brothers Glaucon and Adeimantus, finding this point of view disturbing but difficult to refute, ask Socrates to put Thrasymachus in his place. Socrates with typical banter replies that he would rather shave a lion than rob Thrasymachus of his opinion and then leads the group in search of their definition.

They agree that most people act justly for shallow reasons. Adeimantus recalls that parents and tutors are for ever exhorting children to be just, not for the sake of justice or virtue in itself but in order to preserve their reputation in the eyes of their neighbours, or in order to make a good marriage or to impress the gods who will, they hope, improve their prospects on earth and earmark greater happiness in heaven. Glaucon attempts to get beyond this cheap motivation of punishment and reward, fear and constraint, and recalls the legend of Gyges the Lydian shepherd who found a ring which made him invisible and by means of which he rose to be king. Suppose two men each found such a ring. Suppose each was then free to act as he pleased without fear of detection or constraint and suppose one acted justly and one acted unjustly without fear of acquiring an evil reputation. How would 'injustice in itself' affect the one and 'justice in itself' affect the other? Furthermore, what would be the outcome if he who acted justly was reputed to be evil and he who was a monster of injustice acquired the reputation of being an honest man? Which would be the happier?

Glaucon and Adeimantus are desperately anxious to do well in this matter of stripping off the 'accidents' to arrive at the 'essence' and they are equally anxious that 'justice in itself' should prove stronger than its opposite. And as they are fearful that neither may be equal to the appointed task, Socrates launches out into the mainstream of the exposition.

In order to isolate justice and injustice, Socrates begins by tracing the growth of the contemporary state from a tribal, closed society. First, necessity creates a division of labour. Men must have food, clothing, housing and utensils and so, correspondingly, some men must become farmers, weavers, builders and smiths. A system of exchange is called into being. Inevitably, a demand for imports will arise in answer to which a whole race of merchants – native and foreign – will swell the numbers of the state and they in turn will be supported by systems of transport with shipbuilders, sailors, navigators, to say nothing of middlemen and financiers.

The group agrees that Socrates has conjured up a state but no one is certain at what point justice and injustice entered it. They proceed then to the next logical phase: the consideration of the luxurious state. 'For,' says Socrates astutely, 'by extending an enquiry to such a state we shall be more likely to see how political justice and injustice originate.' Since men are never satisfied with life's bare necessities, a whole swarm of specialist trades and professions will swell the state to bursting-point: hunters, artists, musicians, poets, entertainers, nurses, barbers, cooks, confectioners and makers of cosmetics. Doctors will be far too heavily in demand. By now the state has too many mouths to feed; it needs more land. But its neighbour has been evolving similarly; not only will it not cede territory, it is bent on acquisition. The whole company quickly sees the familiar pattern which leads to war and Socrates says that whether war is good or evil it has its origin in that which causes most individual and public evil: appetite and the acquisitive principle.

Up to this point the development of the ideal state has coincided with common practice. But now the first planned Utopian element is introduced. A standing professional army will be trained which will guard the city like well-bred watch-dogs – alert, swift and strong. The principle of the division of labour must be consistently maintained. The sculptor must stick to his chisel, the barber to his scissors, the cobbler to his last and the soldier to such skills as enable him to 'guard' the state. Here must be no breath of amateurism, no loop-hole for inefficiency, no tendency towards weakness. The Guardians must be fierce towards enemies, gentle towards friends. They must possess in full the power of discernment and who but the trained philosopher possesses this to any high degree? 'How then,' asks Socrates, 'are these Guardians to be brought up and educated?' He hints that an enquiry into the ideal system of education for the Guardians may even lead the company towards their goal of the isolation of justice and injustice.

In the historical Athens of Plato's day education for boys consisted of gymnastics for the body, and all the arts presided over by the

Muses for the soul. It was, of course, a purely private affair. These subjects will continue to form the basis of a young Guardian's education but the state will provide it and closely supervise its form and content. Impressionable children must come in contact only with such legends, myths and literature as ennoble the mind and make it fearless. No Guardian is to be infected with tales of quarrels among gods, or transformations of gods into less exalted creatures, or mourning or fear of death or the levity of immoderate laughter. Accordingly, much of Homer and Hesiod will have to be expunged. Truthfulness must be valued highly and inculcated by every means. If any lying or deception has to be practised, that must be a privilege residing solely with the Rulers for the benefit of the body politic just as the right to prescribe drugs resides in the hands of the physician.

The principle that one man cannot play many parts must be rigidly applied. It will not therefore be possible for a young man to undertake the role of tragic or of comic actor. A Guardian must at all times concentrate on defending his state, on attaining to physical and moral perfection. To imitate a diversity of characters would quite undermine his training. Far worse! He would have to portray, convincingly, weak, sordid qualities. What could be more dreadful than a Guardian 'thinking himself into' the part of a woman or a slave! The company agrees that just as their Republic will not tolerate a shoemaker in command of a ship or a joiner leading a jury or a sausage-maker fighting as a soldier, neither will they permit to remain within their borders 'an individual clever enough to assume any character and give imitations of anything and everything'.

Music plays an important part in training but there must be a strict censorship to ensure that only rhythms and harmonies conducive to the training of warriors are heard in the state. The Ionian and Lydian modes were sloppy and effeminate and could not be allowed to co-exist with Guardians. The manly Dorian mode was to be favoured. (We recall that Lycurgus was said to have visited Ionia to see how his Spartans should *not* live.) The growth of any kind of luxury or effeminacy in the arts must be made impossible, says Socrates: 'Then we must not only compel our poets, on pain of expulsion, to make their poetry the express image of noble character; we must also supervise craftsmen of every kind and forbid them to leave the stamp of baseness, licence, meanness, unseemliness on painting and sculpture, or building, or any other work of their hands; and anyone who cannot obey shall not practise his art in our commonwealth. We would not have our Guardians grow up among representations of moral deformity, as in some foul pasture where, day after day, feeding on every poisonous weed they would, little by little, gather insensibly a mass of corruption in their very souls.'[1]

To this carefully fostered culture will be wedded a strict and simple regimen of physical education. For the company is agreed that whereas unadulterated physical education would tend to produce unimaginative, boorish youths, a preoccupation with the arts would result in flabbiness of sinew and muscle. The proper blend of each will produce a Guardian with a nicely balanced, harmonious soul. Socrates cannot subscribe to the idea – so constant a caption in our educational press – of 'Mens sana in corpore sano'. Rather, in his opinion, does the philosophic soul 'have the power to make the bodily condition as perfect as it can be'. He remarks cuttingly that half the energy of doctors is ill used, not in curing genuine disease 'but because, through living in idleness and luxury, our bodies are infested with winds and humours, like marsh gas in a stagnant pool, so that the sons of Asclepius (doctors) are put to inventing for diseases quite ingenious names as flatulence and catarrh'. Socrates was forever drawing on his observations of artisan life around the Agora of Athens. His remarks have a down-to-earth ring when he says that a busy carpenter has no time to indulge in imaginary illness or to be coddled by doctors. If he is advised to have 'complete rest' he returns to work and by regaining his health or losing his life he finds a solution of his problem.

The education of the Guardians to the age of twenty having been settled we now consider a third element, the coping stone of the political structure: the Super-Guardians or Rulers. These will be recruited from those Guardians who have shown the greatest aptitude for intellectual and manly leadership and who have proved their philosophic qualities in the severest tests imaginable. As professional philosophers they will, of all members of the Republic, approach nearest to the eternal Forms of Goodness, Truth and Justice. They, and they alone, will have the requisite knowledge to command. The Guardians will continue to act as watch-dogs of the state in an 'auxiliary' capacity to the Rulers. The orders of the state will take the form of:

[1] *The Republic*, trs. F. M. Cornford, p. 87 (Oxford).

(1) *Rulers*   :   legislative and deliberative
(2) *Guardians or*
    auxiliaries :   executive
(3) *Craftsmen*   :   productive

At this point Socrates becomes unusually hesitant. He knows of a cement which he hopes might indissolubly bind the several elements of his state. It is no material cement; it is purely psychological, yet real – the power of belief accepted. What is this belief and how can it be made acceptable? His friends encourage Socrates to proceed but editors and translators hold us up to ensure we do not misunderstand the meaning of *pseudos gennaion*. Are we to call this a 'bold flight of invention', a 'noble lie', or a 'fine falsehood'? Call it what you will the substance of it was: (*a*) The whole community must be induced to a belief that their upbringing and training on earth was but a dream. In reality all have been maturing together in the common womb of mother earth until the state was ready and have been sent up to the light of day at the appointed time. 'So now they must think of the land they dwell in as mother and nurse, whom they must take thought for and defend against any attack, and of their fellow citizens as BROTHERS BORN OF THE SAME SOIL.'

(*b*) Although all indeed are brothers, the god who fashioned them mixed gold into those fit to rule, silver into those who could defend and brass and iron into those who worked by hand, the farmers and the artisans. A prophecy will be put out that ruin will overtake the state if ever it passes into the hands of men of the baser metals.

The framework of the state is now:

(1) *Rulers*   :   legislative   :   gold
(2) *Guardians or*
    auxiliaries :   executive   :   silver
(3) *Craftsmen and*
    farmers   :   productive   :   brass and iron

Should any unfortunate mutations occur – and such an eventuality must be envisaged – the machinery for upward or downward transfer must be set in motion without regard to sentiment; the tripartite nature of the community, for all the brotherhood and consanguinity of its members, must be preserved.

Our state will now be superior to all others. It will be wise, for it is ruled by professional philosophers. It will be brave and strong, for its Guardians have been bred and trained to be so. It will be united, for there will be no disparity of riches to upset that equilibrium with which the state began. To ensure complete equality in material things, and therefore unity, the Rulers and the Guardians will live communally having no contact with silver, gold or private property. They will be content with the silver and gold which god has implanted within them. There is no doubt that Plato sees the success or failure of his state residing in the continued unity of the whole ruling group, i.e. Rulers and Guardians. It is equally clear that anything which might cause division must steadfastly be excluded. Any intrusion of property, silver or gold, would, like the injection of bacteria, set up disease and decay and ferment within a few generations. Was not after all Timon a fellow citizen and contemporary of Plato's? Was he not making the same point in a more personal way by fleeing from a society made detestable by wealth? Of the 'yellow, glittering, precious gold' he says:

> Thus much of this will make black, white; foul, fair;
> Wrong, right; base, noble; old, young; coward, valiant.
> Ha, you gods! Why this? What this, you gods? Why, this,
> Will lug your priests and servants from your sides;
> Pluck stout men's pillows from below their heads;
> This yellow slave
> Will knit and break religions, bless the accursed,
> Make the hoar leprosy adored, place thieves,
> And give them title, knee and approbation,
> With senators on the bench: this is it
> That makes the wappened widow wed again,
> She whom the spital-house and ulcerous sores
> Would cast the gorge at, this embalms and spices
> To the April day again.[1]

Clearly this stuff has no place in a Utopian state. Love of gold, however, even if it is the most powerful and widespread agent of disunity and decay, is not the only one. Plato makes it clear that unless selfish, acquisitive, individual and family pride can be subordinated to the interests of the Ruler-Guardian section as a whole, disunity and disintegration will bring it down. Hesitatingly and with diffidence – assumed or real – Socrates proposes a revolutionary scheme which is not so much designed to abolish the family as a

[1] Shakespeare: *Timon of Athens*, Act IV, Sc. 3.

unit of the society, although it does do that, but to make the family
co-extensive with the Ruler-Guardian section of the state.

First of all women will take their place as watch-dogs and Guardians
of the state, and, if they are to play their part fully, they must have
full equality of training and education with the men. It is only
common sense that Guardians should have both wives and mothers
who can share and understand their work. Once both sexes have
been made physically and philosophically robust, care must be taken
to ensure that all unions are arranged on strictly eugenic lines. The
Rulers will draw up the list of unions in advance: 'It seems', says
Socrates, 'they will have to give their subjects a considerable dose of
imposition and deception for their good. We said, if you remember,
that such expedients would be a useful sort of medicine.' Then
certain festivals would be instituted at which the selected couples
would be paired off in marriage, ostensibly according to a system
of drawing lots, but in reality according to the lists drawn up in
secret by the Rulers.

The healthy children of these unions will be reared by trained
nurses in crèches in a separate quarter of the city. Children of inferior
(though Guardian) parents and inferior children 'will be hidden
away, in some appropriate manner that must be kept secret'. Parents
and children will not be known to one another. Thus parents will
accept an extended responsibility for all children; children will be
more fortunate and secure in that they may call upon all the adults
of the state as parents.

It must be emphasised that this is no demoniac plan on Plato's
part to deracinate affection from the hearts of his citizens. It is, in
his opinion, vital to the cohesion and survival of his state. It is only
in a city so ordered that the Guardians 'will not rend the community
asunder by each applying the word "MINE" to different things and
dragging off whatever he can get for himself into a private home,
where he will have his separate family, forming a centre of exclusive
joys and sorrows. Rather they will all, so far as may be, feel together and aim at the same ends, because they are convinced that
all their interests are identical.' The Ruler-Guardians, to whom
alone these stringent regulations will apply, will have those irk-
some, onerous family problems – well known to all Athenians –
lifted from their shoulders, and, 'rid of all these cares, they will live
a more enviable life than the Olympic victor, who is counted happy

on the strength of far fewer blessings than our Guardians will enjoy'.

Our imaginary Republic is now launched with its three 'orders' each displaying the appropriate virtues and each functioning with balanced harmony. The Pythagorean Music of the Spheres, as it were, has been made captive and brought down to earth. Socrates has led his followers to the point where justice can be defined, though there is more to be said. Not only is each 'order' fulfilling its appointed duty in the state, but each individual is carrying out the task for which he has been trained, *and no other*. Any encroachment on the part of group or individual would constitute injustice. 'And, conversely,' says Socrates, 'let us repeat that when each "order" – tradesman, Guardian, Ruler – keeps to its own proper business in the commonwealth and does its own work, that is justice and what makes a just society.' The conclusion of Anaximander and Heracleitus, that there is a cosmic justice which limits acts of encroaching in nature, has been transferred by Plato to society. But Plato faces a problem from which these Ionians were free. Man can contemplate the elements and their conflicts with a considerable degree of impartiality if not accuracy. He can stand aside and formulate laws by observation. No man, however, can stand aloof as he contemplates the society in which he lives and has his roots. Linked to events by bonds of strong emotion, how can a statesman analyse with objectivity what is really taking place, much less, with justice, legislate for events to come? How can he measure that of which he is a part – and an interested part at that? How, in this life of flux and fusion and intractable emotions, can man find a fixed framework of reference? Is it not obvious that to have Everyman, at the dictates of his tastes and appetites, tugging at the wheel is bound to head the ship of state for doom? And even if a well-meaning politician tries to steer, is he not as ineffectual as a pilot who tries to navigate by the light of a feeble lamp bobbing up and down on his own mast-head?

There is a way. There is a bright, fixed star. The way is the way of philosophy, the star is the Idea of the Good. Far more vital to Plato than the definition of justice in the state is the creation of the philosopher who must bring to being the ideal state and govern it. For this demands a definition of justice in the soul. It provides the answer to the second question posed at the outset of the whole debate. How does justice in itself, with all external systems of punishments and rewards removed, affect the individual?

It is at this point, therefore, in the Dialogue that Plato introduces his, by now, fully-fledged theory of Ideas or Forms ending up with the allegory of the cave as described in the last chapter. He outlines the kind of curriculum which would mould young men of twenty years and upwards into philosophers and which would lead them towards knowledge of the Ideas. In this curriculum mathematics plays a major role and we can fairly safely assume that it bears a close relation to the education received by young men in Plato's Academy. A few points are worth noting. The arithmetic taught must not have a commercial bias but must deal, rather, with the theory of number. Geometry is most important because it directs the soul upward to grasp eternal and incorporeal things, i.e. geometrical forms and their relationships. Socrates admits the value of astronomy in the curriculum provided it takes the form of a series of geometrical problems. It must not degenerate into mere physics dealing with material bodies, for the entire direction of our exercise is away from 'the vegetable universe'. Socrates deals somewhat acidly with those who spend their time gazing at the starry heavens in the hope of learning something. They are, after all, falling into the unphilosophic trap of assuming that sense-perceptions of sensible objects are in some way connected with knowledge. Why, a man might as well go down on his back and contemplate a painted ceiling and imagine he was aspiring to wisdom by the mere act of looking upwards!

This brings us to the 'coping stone' of Plato's educational edifice, the discipline which draws the soul towards the knowledge of the Good just as the ascent from the cave drew the prisoner to the contemplation of our sun. 'So here, the summit of the intelligible world is reached in philosophic discussion by one who aspires, through the discourse of reason unaided by any of the senses, to make his way in every case to the essential reality and perseveres until he has grasped by pure intelligence the very nature of Goodness itself. This journey is what we call DIALECTIC.'

Now, at last, even the most hesitant of the group can see not only what justice and goodness are and the nature of the soul's journey to them, but they can see that to ask why a man should choose justice rather than its opposite is as pointless as asking why the prisoner wishes to remain in the sunlight.

Plato's problem is our problem. Death and debasement of human values were as absolute for the Greeks as they are for us. We may not find it possible to go along with Plato, we may find some of his ways distasteful or even repugnant; it may be true that he begs the question as often as he answers it. But at least he put the problem clearly – for the first time since civilised communities arose – in his famous paradox and no question can be answered until it has been put: 'Unless either philosophers become kings in their countries or those who are now called kings and rulers come to be sufficiently inspired with a genuine desire for wisdom, unless, that is to say, political power and philosophy meet together, there can be no rest from troubles for states, nor yet, as I believe, for all mankind.'[1]

[1] *The Republic*, trs. F. M. Cornford, p. 174 (Oxford).

CHAPTER XIV

Plato (3). The Laws

Poetry fettered, fetters the
Human Race.

The Gods of Egypt and Greece were
Mathematical Diagrams – see
Plato's Works.

WILLIAM BLAKE

When introducing his *Essay Concerning Human Understanding* in which he argued against the possibility of the existence of innate ideas, John Locke wrote:

I have been told that a short epitome of this treatise, which was printed in 1688, was by some condemned without reading, because innate ideas were denied in it: they too hastily concluding that, if innate ideas were not supposed, there would be little left either of the notion or proof of spirits. If anyone take the like offence at the entrance of this treatise, I shall desire him to read it through; and then I hope he will be convinced that the taking away false foundations is not to the prejudice, but advantage of truth, which is never injured or endangered so much as when mixed with, or built on, falsehood.

At this point one must, like Locke, appeal to the reader to investigate for himself or herself the writings of Plato. For Plato constitutes a gigantic paradox; and whereas discourse upon paradox may, or may not, be entertaining, it is never as enlightening as burrowing to the heart of the paradox by oneself. But not only is Plato an intriguing paradox; as with John Locke's attack on innate ideas, Plato evokes profoundest and most contrary reactions not only at different times and in different people but at the same time and within the same person. Consider, for example, the judgment of Sir Maurice Bowra writing just thirty years ago:

Plato was one of the most gifted men who ever lived, a thinker of great originality and power, for whom nothing was too difficult and nothing to be shirked, a stylist of incomparable range and charm, a prose-poet and a master of narrative. His influence on posterity has been incalculable. . . . But at times it is hard not to feel that his life was a gigantic mistake, that he was deluded into substituting a lifeless mirage for the world of flesh and blood, that his great arguments are based ultimately on the passions and especially on fear. . . . He attacked the arts with the fury of a great artist and fought poetry with its own choicest weapons.[1]

In any consideration of Plato today it is particularly interesting to note that those who, while fully aware of the magnitude and relevance of Plato's aims and achievements (if one may say so without presumption), make the most sustained attack upon him are writers who are more than usually interested in the science and politics of the twentieth century, e.g. R. H. S. Crossman, Dr Karl Popper and Bertrand Russell. In the final paragraph of the addenda to the most recent edition of his volume *The Open Society and its Enemies: The Spell of Plato*, Dr Popper is at pains to point out:

Yet I do not wish to end this long discussion without reaffirming my conviction of Plato's overwhelming achievement. My opinion that he was the greatest of all philosophers has not changed. Even his moral and political philosophy is, as an intellectual achievement, without parallel, though I find it morally repulsive, and indeed horrifying.[2]

Similarly vigorous language is used by R. H. S. Crossman in introducing his *Plato Today*. He writes:

Since the war it has become quite fashionable to pull Plato off his pedestal . . . my senior colleagues [in the faculty of Philosophy at Oxford] were appalled at the notion that the Academy was really a school for counter-revolutionaries and *The Republic* not a timeless exposition of ultimate truths, but a handbook for aspiring dictators.[3]

As in Homeric times battle raged around the body of a fallen hero of either side, so for the past three decades philosophers, as far as

[1] C. M. Bowra: *Ancient Greek Literature*, pp. 188-9 (Home University Library, Oxford).   [2] Vol. I, p. 335 (Routledge).
[3] Introduction, p. 1 (Allen and Unwin).

Plato is concerned, have been locked in conflict, and mainly over the body of ideas contained within the covers of *The Republic*. Need anyone be surprised that a dissertation assuming an air of dogma and authority and involving, as does *The Republic*, education and art, censorship and sex, property and privilege, social structures and social values, engenders disputes both acrimonious and exciting?

No one reads Plato and remains unmoved. It is not without significance that the sub-title of Dr Popper's first volume on *The Open Society and its Enemies* is 'The Spell of Plato'. And so, since of all the Greek philosophers we have been considering, Plato is the first whose writings have survived, and since good and inexpensive translations are now available, one must have recourse to Locke's suggestion and urge that some of them, at any rate, be read: *The Apology* for the picture of Socrates which we believe to be authentic, the Shavian gad-fly goading the citizens and awaiting from them and Anytus the final slap; *The Crito* and *The Phaedo* for Plato the persuasive philosopher and dramatist, and for that incomparable final exit of Socrates; *The Phaedrus* and *The Symposium* for 'the spell', 'the stylist of incomparable range and charm', and 'prose-poet' and 'master of narrative whose influence on posterity has been incalculable'; *The Republic* and *The Laws* for the extended essence of the Platonic system, for the inaugural debate on those very problems which are concerning us vitally today. Perhaps one might add *The Parmenides* to witness Plato calling in question no less a thing than his central theory of Forms, and for the somewhat negative experience of grappling with Plato in one of his later moods of somewhat grim obscurity.

In any attempts to see Plato in perspective there are two concepts which we have to regard as fundamental: the concept of the eternal unchanging Forms, and the concept that knowledge of those Forms was attainable for certain philosophically-minded mortals who were prepared to submit to the rigours of a carefully prescribed discipline. Those who were either unable or unwilling to pursue this curriculum were automatically disqualified as serious candidates in the search for Truth. Further, only knowledge of the Forms or Universals was worthy of the name of knowledge. Acquaintance with the various particulars, the manifold and relatively ephemeral objects and experiences which were but shadowy and imperfect reflections of the Universals could not properly be classified as knowledge. On these

concepts Plato staked all; so we must consider how they played
their part in the body of Platonic doctrine and how they have been
responsible for the criticisms of Plato which have been quoted. But
first we must take another look at the times in which those doctrines
were formulated, the problems to which these were Plato's answer
and the way in which preceding philosophers exerted their influence
on them.

Plato's long life coincided with the passing away of Athenian independence as a city state. He was born at a period in the Peloponnesian War which was marked by unprecedentedly bloody acts of
violence and cruelty. As revolution and counter-revolution appeared
on the Greek scene we can appreciate something of the prevailing
atmosphere by noting the language used by Thucydides to describe
the period:

> To fit in with the change of events, words, too, had to change
> their usual meanings...; any act of moderation was just an
> attempt to disguise one's unmanly character; ability to understand
> a question from all sides meant that one was totally unfitted for
> action. Fanatical enthusiasm was the mark of a real man....
> Anyone who held violent opinions could always be trusted, and
> anyone who objected to them became a suspect....
>
> Love of power, operating through greed and through personal
> ambition, was the cause of all these evils. To this must be added
> the violent fanaticism which came into play once the struggle had
> broken out.... Here they were deterred neither by the claims of
> justice nor by the interests of the state; their one standard was the
> pleasure of their own party at that particular moment.... As for
> the citizens who held moderate views, they were destroyed by
> both the extreme parties, either for not taking part in the struggle
> or in envy at the possibility that they might survive.
>
> As a result of these revolutions there was a deterioration of
> character throughout the Greek world.... As a rule those who
> were least remarkable for intelligence showed the greater powers
> of survival.[1]

These are weighty and unpleasant words, and if read in conjunction with Pericles' Funeral Oration they reveal a sad and significant
reversal of civic standards in Athens – even when necessary allowances
are made for any idealising bias on the part of Pericles and Thucy-

[1] *The Peloponnesian War*, pp. 209-10 (Penguin).

dides. And when hostilities eventually ceased, power was collected into the hands of a group of aristocratic extremists – known as the Thirty – motivated by just that breed of factious spirit and lust for revenge and power which Thucydides has described. They were inimical to democracy, heedless of the city's welfare and contained within their number Plato's uncle, Charmides, and his cousin, Critias.

The Thirty, however, did not retain power for long. The democrats returned and the next swing of the pendulum is best described in Plato's own words:

> In these unquiet times much was still going on that might move one to disgust, and it was no wonder that, during the revolutionary changes, some took savage vengeance upon their enemies; but on the whole the returning exiles (democrats) showed great moderation. Unfortunately, however, some of the men in power, brought my friend Socrates to trial on an abominable charge, the very last that could be made against Socrates – the charge of impiety.[1]

During the years which followed the death of Socrates, Plato travelled abroad and visited, among others, three places which were to have an importance in the moulding of his philosophy: Egypt, the court of Dionysius I, despot of wealthy Syracuse, and Tarentum, in Southern Italy, where Archytas, geometer-politician, was not only head of the Pythagorean Brotherhood, but was actively engaged in applying their principles to the administration of the city. The contrast between the passionate, violent and hedonistic court of Dionysius and the Pythagorean 'way of life' made an impression on Plato which appears throughout the whole of the remainder of his life, and which was crucial to all his thought.

It is worth recalling Plato's own description of his state of mind prior to this visit to Sicily and Italy:

> When I considered these things [the behaviour of his relatives and the execution of Socrates] and the men who were directing public affairs, and made a closer study, as I grew older, of law and custom, the harder it seemed to me to govern a state rightly. Without friends and trustworthy associates it was impossible to act; and these could not readily be found among my acquaintance, now that Athens was no longer ruled by the manners and insti-

[1] *The Seventh Epistle*, trs. F. M. Cornford (Oxford).

tutions of our forefathers; and to make new associates was by no
means easy. At the same time the whole fabric of law and custom
was going from bad to worse at an alarming rate. The result was
that I, who had at first been full of eagerness for a public career,
when I saw all this happening and everything going to pieces,
fell at last into bewilderment.[1]

And then with words reminiscent of those in *The Republic* Plato
continues:

At last ... I was driven to affirm, in praise of true philosophy,
that only from the standpoint of such philosophy was it possible
to take a correct view of public and private right, and that accordingly the human race would never see the end of trouble until
true lovers of wisdom should come to hold political power, or
the holders of political power should, by some divine appoint-
ment, become true lovers of wisdom.[2]

So it was that Plato found himself excluded from any form of direct
political participation in Athenian life. But Plato had deep roots
stretching far into the past of Athenian society. Not only was he
connected to the leading aristocratic families but was said to trace
his ancestry through Solon to an early king of Athens and eventually
to the god Poseidon. Living as he did in a period of violent upheaval,
of troubled transition from the easy confidence of the old to the uncertainties of the new, and given both an artistic and philosophic
temper, it is not surprising that Plato forged the philosophic anchor
of the Forms. In spite of late antipathy to Platonic gods and mathematics, William Blake, likewise appalled at the heartless ethos of a
new and a commercial age cried out in one of his prophetic books:

Whatever can be created can be annihilated:
          Forms cannot:
The oak is cut down by the axe, the lamb falls by the
          knife,
But their Forms eternal exist for ever. Amen.
          Hallelujah!

In Athens the old order was passing; Heracleitus' dictum 'Everything is in flux' was painfully apparent; but the 'Forms eternal exist
for ever'.

When it is more than usually obvious that 'the manners and insti-

----
[1] Ibid.   [2] Ibid.

tutions of our forefathers' are dead or without adequate foundations, men seek urgently for some fixed frame of reference, some abiding standard by which to measure right and wrong. Men are searching for just such a frame of reference today. How contemporary sound the strictures of the elderly Plato when he says in *The Laws*, 'Hence our epidemics of youthful irreligion – as though there were no gods such as the law enjoins us to believe in.'

Perhaps we have worked round by a somewhat circuitous route to those criticisms of Plato set out at the beginning of this chapter; but it is in order to get to grips with these indictments that we have, in part, retraced the path which led Plato to the Grove of Academus and the founding there of his Temple of the Muses.

The Republic is a completely authoritarian state. The degree of authoritarianism can only be justified on these assumptions:

1. That there do exist the Forms of such things as Goodness, Truth, Justice, Beauty.
2. That these Forms are knowable to men of philosophic temper who undertake a prescribed course of training.
3. That, as a corollary from No. 2, such men as shoemakers, ship-builders, flautists and vine-growers are denied all cognisance of the Forms.

So much is dependent upon the existence of the Forms as Plato envisaged them and so much of his meticulously planned systems of education is what it is precisely because the Forms are what he believes them to be. But what if the Forms are a delusion? Or what if the Forms exist but are by their nature as likely to be apprehended by a shoemaker, a shipbuilder, a flautist or a vine-grower as by a geometer-philosopher? And whether the Forms exist or not, do they justify the highly illiberal, severely puritanical government of the Republic and the frightening inquisition, heresy-hunting and altogether facile death penalty at the hands of the God-fearing Council of Mathematicians as outlined in *The Laws*?

Now, whatever contemporary Athenians thought, whatever we today think about the Forms, it must be pointed out that Plato himself began to experience some difficulty with the theory after he had completed *The Republic*. In a famous – one might almost say notorious – dialogue called after Parmenides, we catch a glimpse of the difficulties Plato was wrestling with. In this dialogue the fact that

Socrates appears in a junior role and is subjected to a rather severe interrogation by the aged and somewhat awesome Eleatic philoso- phers, Parmenides and Zeno, probably indicates some alteration in Plato's philosophic course. The question is put to the young Socrates which every reader puts to himself on first acquaintance with the theory of Forms. He has been holding forth on the doctrine that each individual action and object on earth 'participates' in its corres- ponding Form or Idea in the other world, when Parmenides says:

> Then Socrates, take certain instances which might seem ridiculous – hair, for example, or mud, or dirt, or anything else particularly worthless or particularly valuable. Have you any doubt as to whether there are Forms of such things, distinct from the speci- mens we can handle?[1]

Socrates, aware that he is face to face with the High Priest of Monism, panics a little, as though he can hear the pounding hooves of a great Pluralist herd coming to engulf him and replies:

> Oh no, things of this sort are just what we see them to be. It would perhaps be going too far to posit Forms of such things. On the other hand, there have been times when I have had a niggling suspicion that what is true in one case may be true in all. But I stop short on the brink and take to my heels for fear of falling headlong into an abyss of nonsense and losing myself altogether.[2]

Socrates attempts to work his way out of the difficulty by querying tentatively, 'May not each of these Forms be a THOUGHT, properly located nowhere but in our MINDS?' But this won't do at all, for the Forms could only play their part in Plato's scheme of things by representing ultimate reality anterior to creation and totally in- dependent of human thought.

Having established that the Forms – if they exist at all – must be 'realities in themselves', the problem arises as to how the particulars of this world do in fact participate in them. How, for example, does a terrestrial horse 'participate in' the Ideal prototype? And how, if there exists the Idea of the Good, is it manifest on earth and how can we have knowledge of it? In reply to this question Parmenides launches into a flood of logic which has left many generations breathless. Plato loved to poke fun at the prose writings of the

[1] *Parmenides*, p. 5 (Everyman's Library, Dent).   [2] Ibid.

Ionian philosophers. He makes Socrates say in one dialogue: 'The strength of a Delian diver is needed to swim through the stuff.' Whether one managed to surface successfully or not at the conclusion of *The Parmenides*, the fact is that serious doubt has been thrown upon the existence, nature and possibility of knowledge of the Forms. Plato does not abandon them – for they certainly appear in one of his last works, *The Timaeus* – but gone utterly is the simple doctrine of anamnesis; gone is the Dialectic of *The Republic*; gone utterly is the confident ring of the words we encountered earlier in *The Phaedrus*:

> For a man must have intelligence by what is called the Idea, a unity gathered together by reason from the many particulars of sense. This is the recollection of those things which our soul once saw while following God – when regardless of that which we now call her being she raised her head up towards the True Being. And therefore the mind of the philosopher alone has wings. . . .

Plato is not, of course, to be criticised for altering his opinions. Far from it; what man of long life and enquiring spirit does not? 'The man who never alters his opinion is like standing water and breeds reptiles of the mind,' wrote William Blake. What Plato is arraigned for is that his systems are authoritarian – even unto death – and his authoritarianism is absolute although the grounds for it are shifting and unsure.

Again, throughout *The Republic*, Plato writes as if there were an exact parallel between a flautist learning to perform competently or a shoemaker acquiring the skill to make a good pair of shoes and a philosophic man acquiring knowledge of the Good or an insight into the art of Good Government. But surely any assumption of such a parallel is fallacious. There *can* be agreement among men as to the excellence or otherwise of a pair of shoes; there *can* be agreement among men as to the accuracy and skill of a flautist – there can even be objective physical measurement of the accuracy of any given note; but *can* there be agreement among men as to what is good, what is true, what is just or what is beautiful? Can a citizen 'specialise' in learning Goodness in the way he can specialise in shoemaking, shipbuilding or vine-growing? Or is there more than a little sophistry in classifying all these as comparable skills?

Before moving on from consideration of the place held in *The*

Republic by the Forms, anamnesis and the dialectic which assists the soul in its recollection of its life with the Forms, there is one observation which we may legitimately make. If anyone in his lifetime practised drawing near to the Ideal world and a knowledge of Justice, surely Plato did. If anyone had the will, the ability and the interest to allow anamnesis to operate, surely Plato had. If anyone might have been privileged while still an earth-bound mortal to catch a glimpse of the Ideal City, surely Plato might. Yet when he comes to set down in a book a description of the Ideal City he is not able to say: 'Here is Civitas Dei, my soul knew it when it was with God and daily discipline of the dialectic coupled with anamnesis have restored to me the vision I once knew.' No. He says: 'Here is Civitas Dei. I know it from the constitution established by lawgiver Lycurgus for his Spartans in that dusty settlement in the Eurotas valley and which they manage to maintain unchanged.' Indeed, the great Victorian scholar, Jowett, once described *The Republic* as 'the Spartan constitution appended to a government of philosophers'. And it is important in any appraisal of Plato to see why this should have been so.

Plato thought of creation as an act whereby the universal unchanging Forms gave their imprint to the mortal, earthy and comparatively ephemeral particulars of this world. Not only are all objects inferior to the pure Forms whose stamp they bear, but all change in men and communities from the time of creation onwards is change for the worse. At the time of the creation the gods dwelt with man on earth; it was a 'golden age'. In a late dialogue, *The Statesman*, Plato described that early state of blessedness in these terms:

> Moreover the animals themselves had been allotted, by kinds and herds, to the pastoral care of divinities, each of whom himself provided fully for all the requirements of his charges. And so well did the divinities fulfil their task that there was no such thing as a wild animal, no animal preyed upon another, nor indeed was there war or any kind of hostility throughout the animal kingdom. Such a state of affairs brought in its train innumerable other benefits. Returning, however, to mankind, here is the explanation of their effortless life. They were watched over and tended by the god himself, just as other kinds of animals are looked after by human beings, who are a more god-like race and superior to

them. Under his rule there were no systems of government, and no possession of wives or children; all sprang to life from the bosom of the earth, retaining no memory of their previous existence. Instead they had abundance of those fruits which grow on trees and of other vegetable products, without having to till the soil which yielded them of its own accord.[1]

Since for Plato there had been a 'golden age', an age when man was nearer to God and the eternal Forms, it follows that for him all change, all action of time on societies must be for the worse. This is one reason why we find him enamoured of those very societies which had gone furthest in his day towards arresting change and adopting a constitution guaranteeing the greatest possible rigidity: Crete, Egypt and Sparta. Indeed, one could say with some justice that Plato, after a visit to Egypt, returned to Athens impelled by a belief that it was necessary to embalm the body politic. Just as skilful embalmers could halt corruption in a beautiful body and impart to it a certain quality of fragrance and eternal life, so Plato thought to resist the intrusion into corporate life of mutability and decay. It was to this end that the Guardians in *The Republic* were asked to accept the discipline of such transparent living; it was to this end they were to renounce all claim to private property, to families, to silver and gold; in short to anything which led to thinking in such terms as 'mine' and 'thine'. For 'mine' and 'thine' inevitably becomes 'mine' versus 'thine' and hence come the seeds of division and decay.

Although in the long lapse of years between the writing of *The Republic* and the work of his old age, *The Laws*, Plato had become disenchanted with Sparta and painfully aware of the weakness inherent in its isolated conservatism, the compulsion to create a Utopia with the highest possible degree of fixity remained. In the latter work, as the name suggests, Plato relies on law to stifle all silly preoccupation with novelty or new-fangled fashions of any kind. For example, in speaking of music and his admiration for Egyptian institutions he says:

but in this matter of music, at least, it is a fact, and a thought-provoking fact, that it has actually proved possible in such a sphere, to canonise melodies which exhibit an intrinsic rightness permanently by law. So as I was saying before, if we can but detect the

[1] p. 246 (Everyman's Library, Dent).

intrinsically right in such matters, in whatever degree, we should reduce them to law and system without misgiving, since the appeal to feeling which shows itself in the perpetual craving for novel musical sensation can, after all, do comparatively little to corrupt choric art, once it has been consecrated, by deriding it as out of fashion. In Egypt, at any rate, its corrupting influence appears to have been in no wise potent, but very much the reverse. (Note the thematic words here: canonise, rightness, law, corrupting influence.)[1]

Now what Plato has written here about music epitomises his preoccupation with the establishment by law of complete conformity and fixity of fashion in other spheres in *The Laws*. Education will be taken care of for each individual not merely from birth but before birth. Censorship will be the prerogative of the lawgivers. Foreign travel and intercourse with other states are to be reduced to the severest minimum that can be considered consonant with commercial and diplomatic needs as 'the itch for innovation is caught by host from visitor and visitor from host'. And, irony of ironies coming from an Athenian, and a reputed descendant of Poseidon at that, the new city – whose constitution is the subject of the book – is to be denied access to the sea; for what is more conducive to change and easy commerce of 'the novel' than to be a busy sea-port?

The new Athens is to be shorn of its other great glory too – the civic presentation of dramatic poetry. We read in *The Laws* as in *The Republic* that the dramatic poet is politely but firmly to be escorted to the borders of the state and asked to leave. It may indeed be true for the poet Auden in our modern western world

> For poetry makes nothing happen: it survives
> In the valley of its saying where executives
> Would never want to tamper.[2]

But it certainly was not a point of view to which Plato in his fourth-century Athens could subscribe. In Athens where education was founded on the poets, Homer and Hesiod, and the performances of dramatic poetry in the theatre of Dionysus were not only available to but attended by the majority of the citizens, if 'rightness' was to be 'canonised', then executives would 'want to tamper'; and no doubt Plato thought that one Euripides was quite enough.

[1] *The Laws*, trs. A. E. Taylor, p. 34 (Everyman's Library, Dent).
[2] *In Memory of W. B. Yeats*.

Although in *The Laws* life is more normal and relaxed than in *The Republic*, although the discipline of the dialectic does not appear as such and although the call to mortify the flesh is somewhat modified, in the reading of the later pages of the dialogue one is grimly aware of those 'mind-forged manacles' lurking in the shadows. The Philosopher-Kings or Rulers of the Republic have given way to a body of superior vigilantes, the Nocturnal Council (so named because they meet before day-break), a body of learned and experienced jurists, priests and educationists who are granted the power, and are assumed to possess some knowledge which enables them to 'canonise melodies which exhibit an intrinsic rightness permanently by law'. It is to this body that citizens persisting in non-conformity of belief must surrender their lives. Once again we find the assumption that there exist criteria of rightness, sufficiently objective for a selected group of rulers, to warrant the taking of life. The wheel has come full circle. Plato professes that his life of philosophy was inspired and influenced by Socrates; and now, he proposes a constitution so inimical to individuality that it would have been impossible for a Socrates to have survived a fraction of the seventy years or so which the historical Socrates had lived out in Athens. Indeed the chief heresy which the Nocturnal Council existed to hunt down was precisely one of those on which Socrates was indicted: he did not believe in the gods of the State.

There is a sense in which we could view the whole of Plato's work as a massive dam constructed to halt the flow and action of Time. For him Time was a great enemy. Parmenides with a fine arrogance, if with some lack of realism, ignored Time and its attendant change as illusions practised on poor, mortal senses. Anaximander and Heracleitus knew that a frank recognition of Time's power brought one nearer to reality. Sophocles, nearing the end of a life which spanned a century and seeing the break-up of the city state which was so deeply affecting both Socrates and Plato, paid his tribute to Time in the form of a beautiful ode spoken by the aged and exiled Oedipus:

> Time, Time, my friend
> Makes havoc everywhere; he is invincible.
> Only the gods have ageless and deathless life:
> All else must perish. The sap of earth dries up,
> Flesh dies, and while faith withers falsehood blooms.

> The spirit is not constant from friend to friend,
> From city to city; it changes soon or late;
> Joy turns to sorrow, and turns again to joy.[1]

For Anaximander, Heracleitus and Sophocles Time merely brought change, and the sum total of good or ill might remain constant. In Plato's scheme of things Time, along with creation, had sundered the soul from the eternal Forms to be with which was its nature and its right.

Time, on the other hand, has been tolerant with Plato.

> Time that is intolerant
> Of the brave and innocent,
> And indifferent in a week
> To a beautiful physique,
>
> Worships language and forgives
> Every one by whom it lives.[2]

But if Time has been tolerant, history is catching up with him. The history of the twentieth century does not predispose men to view kindly so authoritarian a state as that portrayed in either *The Republic* or *The Laws*. Modern society is not likely to view with sympathy the tripartite state comprised of men of gold, silver and brass, with effective mobility from group to group precluded and education restricted to a self-perpetuating few.

The inscription over the portals of Plato's Academy enjoined man to know geometry (i.e. to study other-worldliness); Apollo on his portals at Delphi enjoined man to know himself; the present age enjoins man to know himself in the context of the universe in which he finds himself. This is the essence of a scientific age and its methods are deeply at odds with Plato's entire epistemological system. At a time when the very continents are said, literally, to be on the move we can sympathise with Plato's search for a 'solid without fluctuation'. But we must consider whether it is wise to be preoccupied with a hypothetical solid and to fail to understand the fluctuation which is our life.

The poet-philosopher Yeats, who at the outset of his literary career was intent on linking his soul to the Platonic Forms by means of his poetry, eventually wrote:

[1] *Oedipus at Colonus*, p. 90 (Penguin).   [2] W. H. Auden, op. cit.

Those masterful images because complete
Grew in pure mind, but out of what began?
A mound of refuse or the sweepings of a street,
Old kettles, old bottles, and a broken can,
Old iron, old bones, old rags, that raving slut
Who keeps the till. Now that my ladder's gone,
I must lie down where all the ladders start,
In the foul rag-and-bone shop of the heart.[1]

For Protagoras the ladders by which the spirit rises are set up by man in society; for Plato they are let down to man in society by the Forms. In this passage life has forced the poet round to the former's point of view.

[1] *The Circus Animals' Desertion.*

CHAPTER XV

Aristotle (1). The Man and His Works

Solider Aristotle played the taws
Upon the bottom of a king of kings.

W. B. YEATS

A Clerk ther was of Oxenford also
That unto logic haddë longe y-go.

.   .   .   .   .

For hym was lever have at his beddës heed
Twenty bookës clad in blak or reed
Of Aristotle and his philosophye,
Than robës riche, or fithele, or gay sautrye.

CHAUCER

'Aristotle', said Professor J. A. K. Thomson, 'lived as it were in the same house with Plato, but he habitually looked out of a different window and saw a different landscape.' A great deal has been written and spoken about the amount of Platonism, conscious or unconscious, to be found in the teachings of Aristotle. Some hold that he was more deeply indebted to Plato than he realised or acknowledged. Others are of the opinion that Aristotle represents a great advance in comparison with his predecessor who was but fumbling bravely for the Aristotelian formulation of the answers to their common problems. Yet others see in the divergent doctrines of the two, basically divergent attitudes to experience and to the philosophic problems of their day. Before we tackle the doctrines of Aristotle, let us look briefly at the main factors of his life as we know them.

He was born at Stagira, an Ionian settlement in territory ruled by

Macedonia. As his father, Nicomachus, was court physician at Pella to Amyntas II (father of Philip, and grandfather of Alexander the Great), Aristotle was a ritual son of Asclepius, the god of healing. A boy born into the clan of the Asclepiadae would as naturally learn to use his hands and eyes in the act of healing and dissecting as a member of the Homeridae would use his tongue and ears in declamation, instruction and entertainment.

At the age of seventeen or eighteen Aristotle moved to Athens and became a student at the Academy at a time when its Head was engaged in writing his later dialogues and when great emphasis was being placed on the teaching and study of mathematics and astronomy. The young Aristotle impressed his master by his mental acumen. For nearly twenty years he remained in the Academy under the presidency of Plato, studying, teaching and writing.

When Plato died, Aristotle left the Academy and joined some friends in forming a study circle at Assos on the coast of Asia Minor some way south of Troy. Here the little school set up by former members of the Academy was under the patronage of and included as an earnest pupil Hermias, a man of humble origin, who had become ruler of the area and who appears to have been dedicated to the realisation, in at least one small corner of the earth, of government by a Platonic style philosopher-king. After a mere three years at Assos, Aristotle took up residence at the port of Mytilene in the island of Lesbos. It was during these years spent on Aegean shores that Aristotle devoted himself to the study of marine biology which formed the basis of his treatises on living creatures and powerfully influenced him in the criticisms of Platonic doctrine and in the formation of his own. Twenty years' study under the aegis of Plato with its emphasis on geometrical forms, mathematics and the remote celestial spheres was now supplemented by close and detailed work on living organisms with notebook and scalpel.

After a few years Aristotle's work at the station in Mytilene was cut short by an invitation from Philip of Macedonia to take up residence at the royal court as tutor to the future 'king of kings', then thirteen years old. There seems to have been curiously little spiritual contact between pupil and teacher, each temperamentally the antithesis of the other, each destined to become a byword for conquest in his own field. Alexander, however, did retain his tutor sufficiently in mind and in respect to send to his museum in Athens valuable specimens from the fastnesses of Asia. Aristotle, no longer required in Macedonia, returned to Athens in 335 and rented part of the grove of Lycean Apollo. Here he set up his school, the Lyceum, and from the pleasant shady covered walk of the grove, known as the Peripatos, his followers are frequently referred to as the Peripatetics. Here Aristotle instituted an unprecedented centre of intellectual activity: the collecting of maps and manuscripts, the co-ordinated research into natural history and sociological matters, writing, teaching and lecturing. When, in 323, the news came of the death of Alexander, a resurgent wave of anti-Macedonian feeling swept Athens and the ominous charge of impiety was preferred against Aristotle who had been so closely linked with the Macedonian Court. Expressing his reluctance to see the Athenians 'sin twice against philosophy', Aristotle prudently withdrew to Chalcis where he died in the following year at the age of sixty-two.

As a member of the Academy and as Director of the Lyceum Aristotle was a most prolific writer: the full score of works accredited to him in antiquity amounts to some hundreds. His early compositions were dialogues in the Platonic manner which earned their author a reputation as a stylist. Cicero talks of his 'golden stream of language' and Quintilian of his 'smooth eloquence'. But it is not for any such stylistic qualities that Aristotle is studied today, for these dialogues have perished and the later treatises which we know as 'Aristotle' consist mainly of material for lectures and tutorials edited and arranged by other hands. If the entire range of his writings had survived, scholarship would undoubtedly have been spared the labour it has had to expend in reconstructing the intellectual evolution of Aristotle and charting his position vis-à-vis his former master, Plato. However, like the Clerk of Oxenford, we have 'twenty bookës' at least which have come down to us by devious routes and on which the solid and ample fame of Aristotle rests. It is to the essence of these that we must now turn our attention, not considering them so much individually as in associated groups. Aristotle himself thought of the sciences as falling into three natural divisions: theoretical, practical and productive. Logic was not a branch of knowledge but rather the student's indispensable equipment whereby he might arrive at an understanding of the sciences. The reader may find it convenient to have at the outset a list of the main works to which reference will be made.

LOGIC. A group of some half-dozen treatises known since early medieval times as *The Organon*, or Instrument of Thought. The individual works are: *The Categories, De Interpretatione, The Prior Analytics, The Posterior Analytics, The Topics* and *The Sophistic Refutations.*

THE THEORETICAL SCIENCES. This group contains both *The Physics* and *The Metaphysics.* We must note here, however, that as 'Physics' means the study of the Natural Sciences, Aristotle deals with both Biology and Psychology under the heading of Physics. So the main works of this group are:

I. A. *The Physics, On the Heavens, On Coming-to-be and Passing Away, The Meteorologica.*
   B. *The History of Animals, On the Parts of Animals, On the Coming-to-be of Animals.*
   C. *On the Soul* (Psychology).
II.   *The Metaphysics.*

PRACTICAL SCIENCES. *The Nicomachean Ethics* and *The Politics.* As part of the research carried out in the Lyceum Aristotle edited the constitutions of 158 Greek states; all of these save the first, *The Constitution of Athens*, written by Aristotle himself, have perished.

THE PRODUCTIVE SCIENCES. *The Rhetoric* and *The Poetics* (unfortunately incomplete.)

Of all the manifold achievements and areas of scholarship associated with Aristotle, none is more closely associated with him and in none is he accredited with greater powers of originality than logic. In medieval times up till about the year 1200, all that was known of Aristotle in Europe was his work on logic; so, very naturally, this discipline assumed a very special place in medieval education and tended to be elevated to the status of an 'end in itself' rather than the 'means to greater understanding' which its author had intended it to be. Although Aristotle was the father of logic, it does not mean that there were no antecedents to whom he acknowledged his indebtedness. The Pythagoreans and all those who busied themselves with geometry were concerned with axioms and inference as in logic. Zeno, in accepting the premisses of his opponents and showing their alleged error through his method of *reductio ad impossibile* was employing a kind of logic and it was to this method of arguing that Aristotle ascribed the name 'dialectic'. Socrates and Plato, in seeking inductively the essence of a quality like courage by collecting and examining particular instances of it were employing part of the method discussed systematically in *The Organon*. The Sophists, too, gave considerable stimulus to the systematic investigation of the methods of valid and invalid reasoning and in one of the treatises of *The Organon*, *The Sophistic Refutations*, Aristotle deals with some of the fallacies likely to be encountered in those areas of civic life where influence of the Sophists was prominent.

Every branch of learning has its specialised vocabulary and its complement of traditional technical terms, and logic is no exception. We shall only consider these, however, in so far as they are necessary for the understanding of Aristotle as a whole. One such term is 'substance'. In everyday life we are accustomed to a somewhat indefinite use of this word: e.g. Gum is a sticky substance used as an adhesive; or, Honey is a sweet, sticky substance collected by bees. It is essential at an early stage to discover how Aristotle uses this word, not only in his logic but throughout his universe. This brings us to the doctrines of the Categories and the Predicables.

Aristotle's Ten Categories are perhaps more familiar to us as predicates. As Categories each is thought of in isolation, and taken as a whole, they tell us all that we can properly ask about any 'thing':

Category	Example
Substance	Socrates
Quantity	5' 10"
Quality	inquisitive, fearless
Relation	close by, remote
Place	at home, at Piraeus
Time	yesterday
Position	standing, sitting
State	armed, clothed, barefoot
Action (doing what?)	talking, interrogating
Affection (suffering what?)	being reviled, admired

The primary category is substance and without it the others would be meaningless. Aristotle goes on to say: 'Primary substances are most properly called substances in virtue of the fact that they are the entities which underlie everything else, and that everything else is either predicated of them or present in them.' The importance of this concept of substance will become still more evident when we consider Aristotle's attitude to the philosophic problems of his period.

The doctrine of the Predicables explains that when we link up a predicate with its subject in the form of a proposition, the information given us by the predicate about the subject will be:

(1) *Definition*,	e.g.	Man is a rational animal.
(2) *Genus*,	e.g.	Man is an animal.
(3) *Differentia*,	i.e.	That which differentiates man from other subjects within the species.
	e.g.	Man is rational.
(4) *Property*,	i.e.	A predicate which while not indicating the essence (or definition) of a thing, belongs to that thing alone, and is predicated convertibly.
	e.g.	Man is capable of learning grammar.
(5) *Accident*,	i.e.	A predicate which is not one of the above and may or may not belong to some subject.
	e.g.	Man is brave or man is self-indulgent.

Aristotle held that every proposition and every problem is in some way connected with these predicables.

The term 'logic' in the sense in which it is used today was unknown to Aristotle. His terminology for discourse on the methods of reasoning was 'analytics' and the treatise known as *The Prior Analytics* is famous in particular for Aristotle's exposition of the syllogism. 'A syllogism', he writes, 'is discourse in which, certain things being stated, something other than what is stated follows of necessity from their being so.' In more concrete terms the typical Aristotelian syllogism would be:

> A is true of all B.
> B is true of all C.
> Therefore A is true of all C.

Or:

> All men are rational.
> All Greeks are men.
> Therefore all Greeks are rational.

We see here that the syllogism contains three terms and three propositions. In the second version, the first proposition is known as the Major Premiss, the second as the Minor Premiss and the third as the Conclusion. Looking at the first version it is easy to see that the system contains a middle term linking two extremes. Naturally the middle term is of great importance as it is the pivotal point in the chain of reasoning. It will be immediately obvious that in any attempt to arrive at scientific truth it is at least as important that the premisses should be true as that the reasoning should be valid, and it is almost certainly a matter more fraught with difficulty.

Aristotle says that scientific enquiry is always concerned with the search for the middle term. Suppose, for example, we were stationed on the moon and saw the earth occluding the sun's light; we would experience the eclipse; we would ask ourselves why it was taking place and, being on the moon, the cause would be immediately obvious. In this case both the fact and the cause of the eclipse would be perceived almost simultaneously. And knowing the cause is like knowing the universal, the middle term which links the extremes. We shall find that Aristotle has much to say on the matter of cause; he had taken to heart the discovery of his fellow natural scientist, Alcmaeon of Croton, who in the previous century had written: 'Men perish because they cannot join the beginning to the end.'

SUGGESTED READING

Cornford, F. M. *Before and After Socrates* (Cambridge).
Luce, A. A. *Teach Yourself Logic* (E.U.P.).
Ross, W. D. *Aristotle Selections* (The Modern Student's Library, Charles Scribner's Sons, New York). (The standard translations of Aristotle in the Oxford and Loeb Editions are not easily accessible to non-specialist students. This volume of passages selected and introduced by W. D. Ross is invaluable.)
Taylor, A. E. *Aristotle* (Dover Books).

The following works of Aristotle are available in Penguin Classics:

The Ethics, The Politics, The Poetics.
(The last appears under the title: *Aristotle, Horace, Longinus. Classical Literary Criticism.*)

CHAPTER XVI

Aristotle (2). *His Views of Nature*

> Nature makes nothing which is purposeless or doomed to frustration.
>
> His must surely be a careless mind who does not wonder how it is that a small particle of earth, if raised to a height and then set free, should refuse to remain where it was but begin to travel. . . .
>
> ARISTOTLE: *De Caelo*

A careless mind indeed! The questions asked by Aristotle and his contemporaries about gravity have been asked by physicists down the ages: by Galileo, Newton, Einstein, Hoyle and others. As often, the question remains the same; the answers differ. The sum of knowledge grows – largely because of man's increasing control over materials, and increased expertise in experiment and techniques of measurement. As to whether the sum of wisdom increases likewise is by no means a simple matter. Aristotle, at any rate, believed that man grew both in wisdom and in knowledge and that wonder was the mainspring of this process. He writes:

For it is owing to their wonder that men both now begin and at first began to philosophise; they wondered originally at the obvious difficulties, then advanced little by little and stated difficulties about the greater matters, e.g. about the phenomena of the moon and those of the sun, and about the stars and about the genesis of the universe. And a man who is puzzled and wonders thinks himself ignorant (whence even the lover of myth is in a sense a lover of Wisdom, for the myth is composed of wonders); therefore since they philosophised in order to escape from ignorance, evidently they were pursuing science in order to know, and not for any utilitarian end.[1]

[1] *Aristotle Selections*, ed. W. D. Ross, p. 43 (The Modern Student's Library, Scribner).

If the possession of the element of wonder united Aristotle with his predecessors in their attitude to the world of nature we must now consider wherein he differed from them and how he answered the problems they had posed. In the main these problems were: Is there a substrate and if so what is it? Is change (and this includes motion) the great reality or the great illusion? Since we are beset by change, real or illusory, can we attain to any true knowledge of the things of this world or must we, like Plato, have recourse to the universal Forms of another world? In our efforts to acquire knowledge, what part is played by the senses? What part by soul? If other-worldly universal Forms do perchance exist, how can they participate in the objects which surround us? The philosophical scene (and the basic reason for the part played by Aristotle) is most eloquently set by Marjorie Grene in her illuminating *Portrait of Aristotle*:

> It was the changing face of nature, set free from mythological explanations, that started men philosophising. Everywhere there is a rhythm of contrarieties, hot, cold, moist, dry, hard, soft. The philosopher must find a pattern in the rhythm, the order that somehow rises from the sheer contrariness. Things come from an indefinite and return to it, said Anaximander. Change is so unintelligible as to be totally unreal; only the One, eternal and fixed, has being, said Parmenides. It is the number in things, not the things themselves, that are real, said the Pythagoreans. 'By convention hot, by convention cold; by convention sweet, by convention bitter; only the atoms and the void are real', pronounced Democritus. Nothing is, said Gorgias, if it were, we could not know it, if we knew it we could not express it. Aristotle knew all this and lectured on it habitually in the Introductions to his courses. It was always: my predecessors agreed on this; they erred here, they were right there. And the Platonic dialectic of perception and the Forms he knew not only as history but at first hand. If the problem of Parmenides seemed to him antiquated and the problem of Cratylus (the problem of naming things subject to Heracleitean flux) even more irrelevant, this was not because he simply took things in a cabbage-and-kings way as any child might find them. It was because his experience included an aspect sufficiently striking and sufficiently massive to overcome the traditional dialectic of flux and permanence. Things as he saw them sorted themselves out in defiance of the philosophers. . . .

What was this experience? Surely it was the experience of the practising biologist, who can tell a placental from an ordinary dogfish, or the catfish now known as *Parasilurus aristotelis* from the other species, and specify the reasons for his distinctions.[1]

Parmenides and Zeno found that change could not be explained by reason and so denied its reality. Heracleitus had declared that only change was real. Plato, profoundly disturbed because he believed that all change was for the worse and made any theory of knowledge, within terrestrial limits, an impossibility, had recourse to the other-worldly Forms. Aristotle grasped this nettle firmly and activated rather by fascination than by fear made change the basis of his doctrine and formulated a kind of calculus of nature.

If we turn again to Aristotle's discourse on substance and bear in mind that by substance he meant an individual thing such as 'Socrates' or 'Callias' or 'Bucephalus' (Alexander's horse) or this dog, we find he goes on to say:

> The most distinctive mark of substance appears to be that, while remaining numerically one and the same, it is capable of admitting contrary qualities. From among things other than substance, we should find ourselves unable to bring forward any which possessed this mark. Thus one and the same colour cannot be white and black. Nor can the same one action be good and bad. But one and the selfsame substance, while retaining its identity, is yet capable of admitting contrary qualities. The same individual person is at one time white, at another black, at one time warm, at another cold, at one time good, at another bad.[2]

We can see that what Aristotle is doing here is to retain the substance, in the shape of the individual, Socrates, or in the shape of the species, man, as the fixed point, the anchor, while the qualities attributed to the substance are free to ride, to admit of movement.

Aristotle's doctrine of change and movement in substance is worked out by means of a pair of antitheses which are of crucial importance throughout the whole of the Aristotelian system: Matter and Form, and Potential and Actual. We must be careful to understand these terms in the particular sense they bear in this doctrine. A certain effort of abstraction and imagination is called for in understanding what Matter and Form are, for although each is attached

---

[1] *Portrait of Aristotle* (Faber).   [2] Op. cit., p. 7.

to a substance as an aspect of that substance, neither can exist without the other in ordinary terrestrial objects. The Form of Socrates, or of a man, is that which makes him peculiarly what he is, that which makes him respond precisely to what we mean by 'Socrates' or 'man'. The Matter is the basic stuff which makes it possible for the Form to have existence at all. The Matter associated with the Form which together give that peculiar entity Socrates, may be very similar to the Matter which with its associated Form responds to the name Bucephalus. The two things function very differently and have markedly different modes of being. We must be careful not to think of bone, flesh, blood, etc. as Matter in this context. Rather we must conceive of a hierarchy of definable substances each of which is in turn made up of Matter and Form; and however far we descend in the scale of being, we will not arrive at pure un-en-formed Matter. As we ascend the scale of being we will arrive at Form which is not en-mattered, but that is a special case.

Coupled with the concept of Matter and Form in every substance we find that other typically Aristotelian pair, Actual and Potential. 'Typically Aristotelian' because it is here we see the outlook of one deeply immersed in Natural History, of one who has studied with minute care the development of living organisms from embryo to old age, of one who attempts to oppose a dynamic to a static view of things. Aristotle must have pondered frequently on the relationship between the Platonic Forms and the corresponding mundane objects of our sense perception. If the Form of man, for example, was as immutable as it was eternal, how could it ever correspond to the seven ages of man, or the seventy-seven or seven hundred and seventy-seven? How could that which is static 'inform' that which changes from moment to moment? The concept of Potential and Actual is, in part, Aristotle's answer. Matter is potential, embryo is actual; the embryo in turn is potential, the baby is actual; the baby again is potential, the child is actual, and so on. The Potential is eternally moving, eternally changing into the Actual. Equally, Matter is eternally moving into Form.

But although the concept of Potentiality is necessary if change is to be accounted for, some reflection will show that Potentiality in itself is not sufficient to effect the movement. It is important to note that something which *has* realised its Form, that is to say, something Actual must precede the Potential. For example, there must be the father before there can be embryo or child; there must be the oak before there can be the acorn; for Aristotle there is no hesitation in answering the old question: Which came first, the chicken or the egg? 'Man begets man', is Aristotle's dictum. It will be valuable to bear in mind that all movement into Form and into Actuality for the individual takes place within a species which is immutable and abiding for ever.

Time and again Aristotle impressed upon his students that true knowledge was knowledge of causes; that to know that something happens is mere shallowness unless one probes deeper and reveals the reason why. This leads us to a statement of the well-known Four Causes which we find as a recurrent theme throughout the works of Aristotle. Sometimes he illustrates them in action from the familiar things of plant or animal life, sometimes from objects made by man. Let us take by way of example the very famous statue of Zeus in his temple at Olympia. It was made of ivory and gold on a core of wood by Phidias the foremost sculptor of his time. Placed, as it was, in the central shrine of Olympia, the homing centre of the Greeks scattered throughout their colonies, it was the best known and most widely worshipped statue in the ancient world; and it was recorded that no one could look upon it without wanting to become a better man.

Now Plato would have explained that this very solid and material statue was a transient image, a pale reflection of the only reality, the Form, which enjoyed a separate existence. It happened that the statue perished relatively early in history so that, as often, Plato stated a kind of metaphorical truth. Aristotle, however, would have expressed the relation of the statue to reality in terms like this. The statue had come into being through the operation of four causes working simultaneously:

1. *The Material Cause*: the gold, the ivory and the wood.
2. *The Efficient Cause*: the hands and tools of Phidias.
3. *The Formal Cause*: what the thing represents; in this case the figure of Zeus.
4. *The Final Cause*: the purpose and meaning of the thing; in this case the greater glory of Zeus and the improvement of man.

We may notice here that there is a strong similarity between the formal and final causes; and in the case of natural objects, the efficient cause tends to be merged with them. For example, the whole end and purpose of an acorn is to grow into an oak; the form taken by an acorn as it so develops is that of an oak; and the efficient cause, that which gave an acorn the opportunity of taking on the form of an oak was a parent oak. In the case of the statue, the form existed before the statue in the mind of the artist; in the case of an oak, the form was there already in the parent tree.

Each cause plays its part in the process which makes a thing become what it is. But Aristotle feels that some of his predecessors have too often tried to explain phenomena by pointing only to the material and efficient causes. To do this is like trying to account for a house in terms of the bricks and mortar and labourers' hands only, whereas without some plan of the house in the builder's mind and without some purpose in sight no house at all would emerge. Because of his insistence on the importance of end towards which any process advances, the end, indeed, for the sake of which the process takes place at all, Aristotle's system is highly teleological. This does not mean that, in the Tennysonian sense, he assumes

> One God, one law, one element,
> And one far-off divine event,
> To which the whole creation moves.

Even though Aristotle says that Nature and God do nothing without a purpose and although in *The Politics* he gives the impression of believing that plants and other animals are made for man, he does not appear to find the universe revealing purpose or over-all design. What he does stress is that each individual and each species has within it its own true end and that each living thing breeds true.

In their long struggle to understand the phenomenon of change, the Greeks used interchangeably the ideas of movement and change in a way we do not. Aristotle, in making change and motion the basis of much study and exposition, believed that change was to be accounted for by the following scheme:

There are four types of change:

1. Generation and decay, i.e. a change *of* substance.
2. Change of quality,   i.e. a change *in* substance.
3. Change of quantity,   ,,   ,,
4. Change of place,   ,,   ,,

1. occurs when a substance, e.g. Socrates, is born or passes away. 2. occurs when Socrates becomes arrogant or humble, wise or foolish. 3. indicates growth, e.g. Socrates becoming bigger or heavier. Only 4. is motion in the sense in which we are accustomed to use the word. Aristotle also refers to it as 'local motion' and we note that it is only one of four types of change. Movement under this heading may be either rectilinear or rotatory. It is this latter form of motion which Aristotle holds to be prior to the others and eternal. In fact, there never was a time without motion; it has had no beginning and will have no end.

Since the different types of change and motion are located in widely divergent parts of Aristotle's universe, let us turn at this point from discussion of principles to a brief descriptive outline of the cosmos as he viewed it.

The universe is spherical and finite, bounded by the sphere which contains the fixed stars and containing the spherical stationary earth at the centre of all. Within the outermost sphere lies a nest of spheres which as they revolve, carry round the planets and heavenly bodies. The structure and motions of these spheres are highly complex in order to account for the troublesome apparently vagrant courses of the planets. Some idea of the complexity of the mechanics involved is suggested by the fact that Aristotle had to postulate a total of fifty-five spheres.

Within the innermost of these spheres, that which carries round the moon, we have the sublunar regions; here things are subject to generation and passing-away and are compounded of the four elements: earth, water, air and fire. Of these, earth and fire are extremes and have as their nature to move towards the centre and away from it respectively; water and air are intermediate and seek by nature their positions above the earth and below fire respectively. For Aristotle up and down, heavy and light are absolute. That which is heavy seeks the centre, that which is light moves away from it. It is further part of the nature of these elements that on reaching the region intended for them by nature they move no further. These elements are not in themselves eternal but are constantly generated from and passing into each other. In terrestrial regions permanency rests with the species, while the universe as a whole is uncreated and eternal.

We have met the four elements already in Empedocles' scheme but

Aristotle's conception of them is rather more specific. For him they consist of primary matter, which we can never perceive in its pure and isolated form, in conjunction with two pairs of contraries: hot and cold, dry and moist. Mathematically speaking there could be six different couplings of these qualities, but in fact the coupling of opposites does not occur and so Aristotle's scheme is as follows:

> *Earth* : cold with dry (predominant).
>
> *Water* : cold (predominant) with moist.
>
> *Air*   : hot with moist (predominant).
>
> *Fire*   : hot (predominant) with dry.

We note that hot and cold, moist and dry are not found together. There are other contrary qualities but they are capable of being reduced to our prime four and these are not capable of further reduction. Aristotle cannot accept the postulate of a single corporeal and separable substratum, nor can he accept as the components of the elements those right-angled triangles of Plato's *Timaeus*.

From the lunar sphere outwards (i.e. moving from the earth as centre) all consists of a fifth element (*quinta essentia*, quintessence), the aether. The heavenly bodies, once thought to consist of fire, are formed of aether and it is friction generated by their motion which cause them to give forth light and heat. The natural motion of aether is rotatory whereas the natural motion of the four sublunar elements is rectilinear. The spheres and heavenly bodies carried by them are subject to no change but motion which is perfect and everlasting.

The Efficient Cause of all the coming-to-be and passing-away in the sublunar region is the sun's annual movement in the ecliptic. Aristotle says:

> The movement of the whole is the cause of the continuity, and the inclination causes the approach and the withdrawal of the moving body (the sun); for since the distance is unequal, the movement will be irregular. Therefore, if it generates by approaching and being near, this same body causes destruction by withdrawing and becoming distant. . . . The evidence of sense-perception clearly agrees with our views; for we see that coming-to-be occurs when the sun approaches, and passing away when it withdraws. . . .[1]

[1] *De Generatione et Corruptione*, Book II (Loeb Classical Library, Heinemann).

Both regions, those where the deathless aether runs and those where the four corruptible elements undergo their changes, are, according to Aristotle, the proper study of Physics, or Natural Science; for Physics deals with things which have an existence of their own and are subject to any kind of change. Typically, for Aristotle, the net of Physics is cast very wide and typically, too, that which constituted so great a portion of his work is based on change of some sort.

If the movement of the sun in the ecliptic causes the ceaseless ebb and flow of generation and decay of the sublunar tracts, what in turn maintains the sun and the other spheres in perpetual circular motion? This question brings us to the cardinal point in Aristotle's Metaphysics. This is a word which can easily create difficulty for readers in the early stages of acquaintance with Aristotle. Metaphysics (it received its name simply because it was placed by the editors of Aristotle's works *after* the Physics, in Greek *meta ta phusika*) is often said to deal with Being qua Being or true and most real Substance, but these are rather specialised terms and concepts and do not enlighten much. Perhaps it would be helpful to bear in mind the alternative names for this branch of science, First Science or Theology, and to note that it treats of things which have both a separate existence and are *unchangeable*. Now if we recollect the principles laid down earlier in this chapter (1) that change is a form of motion and (2) that motion is always motion from the Potential to the Actual, away from Matter to Form, we must arrive at the position that if there is something with a separate existence which is unchangeable, that 'something' must be entirely at rest, entirely 'actualised', entirely Form without Matter. In Aristotle's cosmos such a being does exist: it is God.

How then does God, a non-spatial and non-material Form, impart movement to the spheres of aether and to the universe as a whole? The answer in the Metaphysics is this:

> There is therefore something which moves them [the first heavens]. And since that which is moved and moves is intermediate, there is a mover which moves without being moved. . . . And the object of desire and the object of thought move in this way: *they move without being moved*. . . . The final cause, then, produces motion by being loved, and by that which it moves, it moves all other things.[1]

[1] *Selections*, p. 108.

But this Unmoved Mover which excites movement in the outermost sphere in the way that the object of love draws something to itself is eternally active. This may appear contradictory since we have stressed that this Being is wholly immaterial and has no part in motion. So we must ask what kind of activity is possible for pure Form; and the answer is 'thinking'. And when we ask what we would think about if our minds were entirely liberated from Matter and were pure Form, the answer must be that we would think about and have knowledge of the Greatest Good, the Highest Truth in the universe. But God is that Greatest Good, that Highest Truth; in the case of God, thinking and thought are one; God's thinking must be turned upon Himself.

A cautionary word may be necessary here lest we should think of the Prime Mover as in any sense a Creator or as one who guides the universe, in the Christian sense, with providential care. In the Aristotelian cosmos Matter, Time and Movement have had no beginning and will have no end, and God is rapt in self-contemplation.

God is not the sole incorporeal being in the universe. Aristotle's tidy cosmic corm of concentric spheres has movement everywhere but void, empty space, nowhere. In order to account for the irregular motion of the heavenly bodies some of the spheres revolve in a direction opposite to that of their neighbours; they cannot then be in contact and the motion cannot simply be transferred from the outermost sphere. But neither can empty space exist between them. In order to account for the movement of the other fifty-four spheres Aristotle had to introduce for each a being which would stand in the same relation to its own sphere as God does to the First Heaven. Precisely what the status of these beings relative to God would have been in Aristotle's mind is not entirely clear. It may well be that the relationship was very nicely expressed by those medieval theologians who thought of all the Movers in terms of God and his Angels.

It is at this point that the question is asked as to whether Aristotle admitted to his doctrine any concept of immortality. This is a matter which is best discussed in relation to Aristotle's concept of Soul, a concept which it would be well to meet before embarking on the Ethics.

The works of Aristotle abound in terms from which peculiar difficulty arises because they are terms which have passed into common currency with us as meaning one thing but were used by him with a different and more specialised connotation. Such a word is Soul.

Every animate thing is made up of Body and Soul. The Soul is not merely the form the thing takes; it is its function; it determines what it DOES. If an axe had soul, said Aristotle, in an effort to clarify his meaning, its Soul would not be either the material or shape; the Soul would be that which the axe has which enables you to cut down a tree with it. Again, more graphically, if the eye were an animal, then sight would be its Soul. Any eye which does not see does not perform its proper function and is no more an eye than a stone or a bit of wood painted to look like one. With so inseparable a relationship between Body and Soul, Aristotle asserts that it is meaningless to ask whether Body and Soul are one, in the same way that it is meaningless to ask whether the wax and the imprint of the signet ring on it are one or separable. More than that, since, for example, the Soul of man is what makes him function as a man and not as a hyena, it is as meaningless to enquire whether the Soul of man could migrate to the body of hyena as it is to conceive of workmen building a house with the instruments of the orchestra. Here we recognise a point of view diametrically opposed to all that was written and taught by Plato and the Pythagoreans on the subject of Soul and its transmigration.

There is a hierarchy of the faculties of Soul just as there is a scale of Nature:

1. *Nutritive Soul*   in all plants
2. *Sentient Soul*   in all animals
3. *Appetitive Soul* }
4. *Locomotive Soul* }   in some animals
5. *Rational Soul*   in man only

The possession of any one of these entails the possession of those preceding it. Man by virtue of his rational Soul is a very long way ahead of the other inhabitants of the terrestrial sphere; but he does belong to that sphere. Suddenly, after impressing upon us that the idea of Soul without body is meaningless, that the two are only separable in a conceptual way, Aristotle tells us: 'But with regard to reason and the contemplative power this is not yet clear, but this seems to be another class of soul, and this alone is *capable of existing separately, as the eternal from the perishable.'*[1] Did Aristotle find it altogether intolerable that man should be no more than one of those 'dull sublunary' things?

[1] Ibid., p. 204.

CHAPTER XVII

Aristotle (3). The Ethics and The Politics

Where-e'er he shines, oh Fortune, gild the scene,
And Angels guard him in the golden Mean!

POPE

The road of excess leads to the palace of wisdom.

BLAKE

Aristotle believed that knowledge could be divided into three branches: (1) theoretical, which was pursued for its own sake because of wonder and which dealt with things which could not be otherwise than they are; (2) practical, which was pursued in order to be able to control the social environment in which man conducts himself and which deals with things which can be other than they are; and, (3) productive, which has to do with the making of useful or beautiful things.

Politics and Ethics are but different facets of the same branch of practical philosophy, for Ethics investigates the end or purpose of human conduct and Politics suggests to the statesmen and educators how that end may be achieved. Like certain other great writers before and after, Aristotle never doubted that man could be greatly assisted towards goodness and salvation by Act of Parliament; nor, however, did he doubt that philosophers would have serious disagreement about the nature of 'the good'. Indeed, having established in the opening sentence of *The Ethics* that 'the good' is 'that at which all things aim', Aristotle goes on to say:

But we can hardly avoid examining the problem raised by the concept of a universal good. One approaches it with reluctance because the theory of 'forms' was brought into philosophy by

friends of mine. Yet surely it is the better, or rather the unavoid-
able, course, above all for philosophers, to defend the truth even
at the cost of our most intimate feelings, since, though both are
dear, it would be wrong to put friendship before the truth. . . .

And there is another puzzle: what advantage in his art will a
weaver or a joiner get from a knowledge of the absolute good?
Or how shall a doctor or a general who has had a vision of Very
Form become thereby a better doctor or general? As a matter of
fact it does not appear that that doctor makes a study even of
health in the abstract. What he studies is the health of the human
subject or rather of a particular patient. For it is on such a patient
that he exercises his skill. . . .[1]

Having levelled these characteristic criticisms at his erstwhile
colleagues of the Academy, Aristotle proceeds to tackle the problem
according to the principles described in the last chapter.

Happiness appears to be the good at which man and all his actions
aim, and to define happiness we must consider in the Aristotelian
way the precise function of man; we must recall what it is that
differentiates him from other beings. Surely it is the possessing and
exercising of a rational soul? The function of man, then, may be
equated with 'an activity of soul which follows a rational principle';
and the function of a *good* man may be equated with 'an activity of
soul which follows a rational principle and is carried out in accordance with goodness or virtue'.

We see then that happiness is an activity, not a state or a disposition.
It is of little avail, Aristotle gently points out, going to the Olympic
Games and *looking* every inch the fastest runner or the strongest
wrestler in the arena. You have to take action and win before any
crown will come to you. But these principles of action are rather
charmingly qualified by the following observations which introduce
an important motif into these works on practical philosophy:

For all that those are clearly right who, as I remarked, maintain
the necessity to a happy life of an addition in the form of material
goods. It is difficult, if not impossible, to engage in noble enter-
prises without money to spend on them; many can only be performed through friends, or wealth, or political influence. There
are also certain advantages, such as the possession of honoured
ancestors or children or personal beauty, the absence of which

[1] *The Ethics,* trs. J. A. K. Thomson, pp. 32, 35 (Penguin).

takes the bloom from our felicity. For you cannot quite regard a man as happy, if he be very ugly to look at, or of humble origin, or alone in the world and childless, or – what is probably worse – with children or friends who have not a single good quality or whose virtues died with them. Well, as I said, happiness seems to require a modicum of external prosperity – thus leading some to identify it with the condition of those who are 'favourites of fortune. . . .'[1]

Since Happiness is an activity of the rational soul carried out in accordance with virtue, it is important to point out that there are two kinds of virtue: intellectual and moral. Of these the former only comes with time and experience and requires instruction and discipline; the latter is the product of habit. Virtuous habits add up to virtuous dispositions and, indeed, Aristotle points out that the word 'ethics' is derived from *ethos* meaning a habit. We are not born with a disposition so loaded as to make us tend towards either the good or the bad in the way that a stone must by natural law fall downward and fire must burn upward. We have to shoulder the responsibility for creating our own character by our own acts.

In order to lay down some useful guide lines to enable his hearers to choose the moral as opposed to the less moral course of action Aristotle here propounds the famous doctrine of 'the mean'. It was a common belief of the time among doctors, trainers and athletes that bodily health was a state wherein those opposite qualities inherent in the elements were in equilibrium. The doctrine of the mean is the application to the activity of the soul of current theory concerning health of the body:

It is in the nature of moral qualities that they can be destroyed by deficiency on the one hand and excess on the other. We can see this in the instances of bodily health and strength. Physical strength is destroyed by too much and also by too little exercise. Similarly health is ruined by eating and drinking either too much or too little, while it is produced, increased, and preserved by taking the right quantity of drink and victuals. Well, it is the same with temperance, courage and the other virtues. The man who shuns and fears everything and can stand up to nothing becomes a coward. The man who is afraid of nothing at all, but marches up to every danger, becomes foolhardy. In the same way the man

[1] Ibid., p. 43.

who indulges in every pleasure without refraining from a single one becomes incontinent. . . . So also temperance and courage are destroyed by excess and deficiency, and they are kept alive by the observance of the mean.[1]

We are not intended here to develop mere mechanical responses to an inflexible formula. Just as Circe told Odysseus that there was a point beyond which she could not advise him and that in spite of the dire necessity to steer a middle way between Scylla and Charybdis he must veer slightly towards Scylla as being the less dangerous of the two extreme evils, so Aristotle says that the choice must be made according to the person's circumstances and having regard to the nature of the extremes involved.

'But if happiness is an activity in accordance with virtue, it is reasonable to assume that it will be in accordance with the highest virtue; and this can only be the virtue of the best part of us.' So there is a higher pinnacle of happiness: that which is scaled by intellectual excellence. The happiness which ensues from moral goodness, much to be desired though it is, is purely human; the happiness which ensues from intellectual excellence is something more. The conclusion which Aristotle reaches in the tenth book of *The Ethics* is that 'contemplation is the highest form of activity, since the intellect is the highest thing in us and the objects which come within its range are the highest that can be known'. Now we can see clearly the link with the Metaphysics and Psychology, for he continues: 'We must conclude then that the activity of God, which is blessed above all others, must take the form of contemplation. And from this it follows that among human activities that which is most akin to God's will bring us the greatest happiness.'

Earlier in his analysis of happiness Aristotle had told us 'Happiness then, the end to which all our conscious acts are directed, is found to be something final and self-sufficient', and 'By "self-sufficient" is meant not what is sufficient for oneself living the life of a solitary but includes parents, wife and children, friends and fellow citizens in general. For man is a social animal. A self-sufficient thing, then, we take to be one which on its own footing tends to make life desirable and lacking in nothing. And we regard happiness to be such a thing.' Clearly, too, moral excellence by its very nature must often have to do with judgments and actions affecting other human beings.

[1] Ibid., p. 58.

Intellectual goodness, on the other hand, reaching its zenith in the act of contemplation, is self-sufficient to a still higher degree. Not only does this activity proceed without reference to other human beings, it exceeds our own merely human capacity and exists at all only by virtue of that portion of the divine which is within us. This is the point at which we mortals approximate most nearly to that which is divine and that which is immortal. It is as though Aristotle, against all the laws of Nature as expounded by himself, had found a way whereby this one terrestrial creature might quit his proper track and wander up among the ethereal, immortal spheres. And this, of course, is highly reminiscent of the reward worked out by Plato for those prepared to undergo his training in dialectic and to 'practise philosophy'.

But at this point Aristotle with characteristic insistence returns to an earlier caveat, a caveat which leads us straight into his *Politics* and which is of importance for their fuller understanding: '... it is commonly believed that, to have happiness, one must have *leisure*'; and, 'but after all the philosopher is human and so will need the added help of external goods'. To ensure this leisure and these external goods for the right people is a proper function of the politician.

In the first book of *The Politics* Aristotle says: 'If then we are right in believing that nature makes nothing without some end in view, nothing to no purpose, it must be that nature has made all things specifically for the sake of man.'[1] All through his teaching on Ethics and Politics he leans very heavily towards a biological and teleological point of view. Nature, he holds, made male and female ineffective until united in the family, the family must be integrated in the community and the community in the state. Man is not self-sufficient; indeed, he is by nature more of a political animal than bees or any other gregarious creature, 'and he who first founded the state was the greatest of benefactors'.

Not only has nature made man a political animal, but she has established a ruler-ruled relationship for different kinds of men so that it becomes possible to assign each person to his appropriate place in society. It is natural and expedient for soul to rule body, intellect to rule appetite, man to rule woman and Greek to rule barbarian. It is from the barbarians, or foreigners, that Aristotle proposes the slave force should be drawn. He is at some pains in the early part of

---

[1] Trs. T. A. Sinclair, p. 40 (Penguin).

The Politics to show that the status of slave is very much in accordance with nature's design:

> Any human being that *by nature* belongs not to himself but to another is by nature a slave; . . .

> It is then part of nature's intention to make bodies of freemen to differ from those of slaves. . . .

> It is clear then that by nature some are free, others slaves, and that for these it is both right and expedient that they should serve as slaves.[1]

We find, indeed, that nature has been at work in a way which is as arbitrary as it is convenient for Greek society, for 'deliberative soul' is inoperative in a female, undeveloped in a child and in a slave is not present at all.

Before examining different possible types of constitution and the criteria by which citizenship is to be awarded, Aristotle feels obliged to criticise some of the basic points in Plato's ideal programme, particularly those points designed to ensure the maximum cohesion of the citizen body. It is Aristotle's view that a state is by nature a plurality and that a sufficient degree of unity may be secured through education. He therefore restores the family to the state, the child to its parents and property to private ownership. He feels sure that any man would prefer to have a real cousin than a son shared in the Platonic fashion; he fears that communal responsibility for children might result in communal neglect. In Aristotle's state, the severity of edict, the Spartan rigour of communal existence and the austerity of human relationships are softened. Far more than his rather Puritan predecessor, he has an eye to the possible rather than the ideal, a greater regard for human psychology, and he had witnessed the spectacular failure of that state whose earlier ideals had found such weighty recognition in the Republic – Sparta. Aristotle is content to leave judgments and decisions to non-specialist citizens in a way which runs quite counter to what Plato advocated. Typical of many of the commonsense and down-to-earth touches in *The Politics* we read: 'Each individually will be a worse judge than the experts, but when all work together, they are better, or at any rate, no worse. Secondly, there are tasks of which the actual doer is not

[1] Ibid., p. 34.

either the best or the only judge, cases in which even those who do not possess the operative skill pronounce an opinion on the finished product. An obvious example is house-building; the builder certainly can judge a house, but the user, owner or tenant, will be a better judge.'[1] We must, of course, bear in mind that this argument concerns citizens only.

But who are and who are not citizens? Here Aristotle's thinking converges with that of Plato; only the wording differs. To be a citizen entails the exercise of certain civic rights and privileges; the exercise of these requires leisure; the pursuit of education requires leisure; the cultivation of the soul requires leisure. But leisure is precisely a commodity which the working classes, the agriculturalists, industrial and commercial classes, have not got. All mechanical workers, the *banausoi*, as they are in Greek, are rigorously excluded, and 'banausic' has passed into our language as a synonym for what is vulgar and in bad taste. We find that Plato's tripartite community persists but stripped of the metallurgical metaphor: 1. Warriors, rulers and generally well-to-do; 2. Agriculturalists; 3. Artisans.

Class 1. and the citizen-body are co-extensive. Classes 2. and 3. are 'prerequisites' for the existence of Class 1. and the state. Plato saw his ideal state in Sparta, Aristotle his in nature. The city, like earth's other organisms, exists at vegetative, animal and rational levels. It is consistently organised to ensure the central statement of the Ethics to be realised: the Good is an activity of the soul and is achieved through contemplation. Only God is capable of pure contemplation but rational man strives towards it. What is Good for man is paralleled in the state: the class of citizens alone can practise virtue and attain the Good.

It was evident to Aristotle, who believed that politics was the art of the possible, that there must always be a grave discrepancy between the governmental practice experienced in Greek city states in historical times and governmental practice as envisaged by philosophers. Because of human weakness and perversity government is almost invariably carried out in the interests of those who govern. Ideally, government should be the means whereby the state as a whole may attain its true end: the Good Life. Of the three possible types of constitution, ideally speaking, each has its attendant perversion each of which was known in Greece in historical times.

[1] Ibid., p. 125.

It is interesting to note the pattern of these constitutions as Aristotle places them for us in order of preference:

Ideal

Monarchy
Aristocracy
Constitutional Republic (or Democracy where government is exercised for the good of the governed)

Historical

Democracy (as found in real life with normal pressure-groups, parties, etc.)_ REMNANT OF PLATONISM !
Oligarchy
Tyranny

If we write the list as follows we see that Aristotle, in commending Democracy adheres to his own doctrine of the Mean: Monarchy Aristocracy Democracy: Democracy Oligarchy Tyranny. He goes on to say that the political equilibrium which democracy can ensure will be further strengthened if, in economic terms, the state is largely composed of middle-class citizens:

> It is clear then both that the political partnership which operates through the middle class is best, and also that those cities have every chance of being well-governed in which the middle class is large. . . .[1]

Unequal distribution of wealth was held to be one of the chief sources of civil strife and revolutions, and the incidence of these was greatly reduced by building your state on the platform of a property-owning, middle-class democracy. Besides, it could be observed that the acquisition of wealth and political power appeared to go hand in hand, so an equable spread of wealth might reasonably be expected to result in contentment and equilibrium.

If a state is to fulfil the functions for which it exists, it must be neither so large as to be unwieldy and peopled with mere ciphers nor must it be so small as to prejudice its chances of survival. There was, therefore, for Aristotle, an optimum size for the ideal state: it must be possible to survey your territory from a hill in a single glance; and it must be possible to communicate with your citizen body in a single assembly. 'It must', he says, 'have a population large enough

[1] Ibid., p. 173.

to cater for all the needs of a self-sufficient existence, but not so large that it cannot be easily supervised.' By 'supervised' he does not envisage a forbidding body such as we met with in Plato's *Laws*, but rather a state of affairs where isolation and anonymity give way to that kind of participation and friendship which generate a corporate spirit in the state.

In aims and outline *The Politics* retains a certain fidelity to Plato's *Republic*, for, after all, both authors were united in their attitude to the Greek *polis*, in their search for knowledge and in their striving for the good life. In detail they were sometimes startlingly different. But nowhere do we find the pragmatic medical tradition of Aristotle more at variance with the rigid dualistic doctrine of Plato than in their treatment of the role of art and in particular dramatic art in a community. Few writers can have emulated Aristotle in making a massive contribution to both science and literature as he did in his treatises on logic, biology and literary creation. *The Poetics*, in spite of its having survived in fragmentary form has long been a point of departure – and it can fairly be said, a stimulating and exciting point of departure – for students of poetry and drama.

It will be remembered that by the time Plato came to write the final book of *The Republic* his artistic experience appears to have been swallowed up by the logic of his dualistic system. Art for him was mere imitation of terrestrial things which were in turn but pale reflections of the Forms. It follows, therefore, that the artist leads us one stage further from the truth than life itself does and two stages away from the Truth or Forms which we should be contemplating. Likewise, it was sinful for an actor to expend his talents on mere imitation of such qualities as courage and nobility (to say nothing of cowardice and depravity) and the admission of such activity into the community was regarded by Plato as a betrayal of philosophic truth. In the course of the argument in *The Republic*, the chief spokesman, Socrates, explains with some little sarcasm that for a poet to reproduce 'the way physicians talk' and for a poet to 'have knowledge of medicine' are two quite distinct things, 'and', he continues, 'there is no record of any poet, ancient or modern, curing patients and bequeathing his knowledge to a school of medicine as Asclepius did'.

Who better to take up this question than Aristotle, a ritual son of Asclepius? And he did so in a way which showed the analytic and

diagnostic brilliance of the true physician. Typical of his encyclopaedic approach to knowledge, he had, with the assistance of his
students, catalogued and studied an immense survey of city constitutions (158 to be precise) and Athenian dramatic tragedies. Realising
the psychological effects produced on men by the restricting forces
of civilised communal life, he concluded that attendance at dramatic
performances was a corporate therapeutic act of inestimable value
to the state. In *The Poetics*, only a brief, tantalising reference to this
doctrine has survived, but in *The Politics* we find a fuller statement:

> Any feeling which comes strongly to some exists in all others to
> a greater or less degree, pity and fear, for example, but also this
> 'enthusiasm'. This is a kind of excitement which affects some
> people very strongly. It may arise out of religious music, and it is
> noticeable that when they have been listening to melodies that
> have an orgiastic effect, they are, as it were, set on their feet, as if
> they had undergone a CURATIVE and PURIFYING treatment. And
> those who feel pity or fear or other emotions must be affected in
> just the same way to the extent that the emotion comes upon
> each. To them all comes a pleasant feeling of purgation and relie f.

The problem was put by another 'Old Polymath' in twentieth-
century scientific terms when Aldous Huxley wrote:

> Man, the multiple amphibian, lives in a mild or acute state of
> civil war. 'The fierce dispute betwixt damnation and impassioned
> clay' is now regarded as the expression of the fact that an ancient
> brain stem is associated with an over-grown, upstart cortex; that
> an endocrine system evolved for survival in the wild is built into
> the bodies of men and women living under conditions of complete
> domestication, in cages of words, within the larger confines of one
> or other of the cultural zoos.[2]

The Pythagorean element in Plato was terribly conscious of the
ferocity of this dispute betwixt evil and good and adopted a restrictive and censorious attitude. The Spartans had their night-
marish, inhuman safety-valve in the form of licensed Helot-hunts.
Athens, whatever its faults and limitations, showed in this as in so
much else the great genius of its communal spirit: it evolved as the
civic instrument of this therapeutic art its theatre. Not only was it
open to all citizens to find a common emotional experience and out-

[1] Ibid., p. 314.   [2] *Literature and Science*, p. 87 (Chatto and Windus).

let in their national theatre, but those of slender means were paid to go. However unconscious a growth was this homoeopathic treatment, Aristotle's conscious comments on it – as far as we have them – reveal a fine awareness and are perhaps of all his writings nearest to us in this post-Darwinian and post-Freudian age.

CHAPTER XVIII

Aristotle (4). His Position in History

From quotations which I have seen, I had a high notion of Aristotle's merits, but I had not the most remote notion what a wonderful man he was. Linnaeus and Cuvier have been my two gods, though in very different ways, but they were mere schoolboys to old Aristotle.

CHARLES DARWIN to WILLIAM OGLE, 1882

We began our consideration of Aristotle by picturing him as a somewhat Janus-like figure having much in common with Plato but presenting in some way a different attitude to the world around them. It has already become clear that this important difference appears to hinge on Aristotle's work in the field of biology. The biological treatises form a very large as well as a very important part of the corpus of his surviving works. Although there is no certainty as to the date of composition of the major works such as *The History of Animals, On the Parts of Animals* and *On the Coming-to-be of Animals*, we might find it helpful towards an understanding of Aristotle's world outlook and special place in Greek thought if we thought of his philosophy as being influenced by three phases of study in natural history. (1) In the early, formative years he was subject to a discipline which was the most highly empirical and the most scientific of the times: Hippocratic medicine. Apprenticed to his physician father he learned to pay strict attention to detail, to use his hands in the arts of dissection and healing and was introduced to the study of embryology, a branch of study which Aristotle found illuminating and was, in turn, illuminated by the acumen of his deductions and observations. (2) In middle life, in the years between his two periods of residence in Athens, he appears to have studied and recorded with great detail the marine life of the lagoons of the Aegean, and (3) during the last phase of his life, as head of the research teams of the Lyceum, Aristotle supervised and inspired a great deal of skilled, scientific work in a wide field of zoological subjects.

In order fully to understand Aristotle's own attitude to the research carried out in this field by himself and his collaborators it is worth looking at what we might call his Credo – even though it is a somewhat lengthy passage:

Of things constituted by nature some are ungenerated, imperishable, and eternal, while others are subject to generation and decay. The former are excellent beyond compare and divine, but less accessible to knowledge. The evidence that might throw light on them, and on the problems which we long to solve respecting them, is furnished but scantily by sensation; whereas respecting perishable plants and animals we have abundant information, living as we do in their midst, and ample data may be collected concerning all their various kinds, if only we are willing to take sufficient pains. Both departments, however, have their special charm. The scanty conceptions to which we can attain of celestial things give us, from their excellence, more pleasure than all our knowledge of the world in which we live; just as a half glimpse of persons that we love is more delightful than a leisurely view of other things, whatever their number and dimensions. On the other hand, in certitude and in completeness our knowledge of terrestrial things has the advantage. Moreover, their greater nearness and affinity to us balances somewhat the loftier interest of the heavenly things that are the objects of the higher philosophy. Having already treated of the celestial world, as far as our conjectures could reach, we proceed to treat of animals, without omitting, to the best of our ability, any member of the kingdom, however ignoble. For if some have no graces to charm the sense, yet even these, by disclosing to intellectual perception the artistic spirit that designed them, give immense pleasure to all who can trace links of causation, and are inclined to philosophy. Indeed, it would be strange if mimic representations of them were attractive, because they disclose the mimetic skill of the painter or sculptor, and the original realities themselves were not more interesting, to all at any rate who have eyes to discern the reasons that determined their formation. We therefore must not recoil with childish aversion from the examination of the humbler animals. Every realm of nature is marvellous: and as Heraclitus, when the strangers who came to visit him found him warming himself at the furnace in the kitchen and hesitated to go in, is reported to have bidden them not to be afraid to enter, as even in that kitchen divinities were present, so we should venture on the study of every kind of animal without distaste; for each and all will reveal to us something natural and something beautiful. Absence of haphazard and conduciveness of everything to an end are to be found in Nature's works in the highest degree, and the resultant end of her generations and combinations is a form of the beautiful.

If any person thinks the examination of the rest of the animal kingdom an unworthy task, he must hold in like disesteem the study of man. For no one can look at the primordia of the human frame – blood, flesh, bones, vessels, and the like – without much repugnance. Moreover, when any one of the parts or structures, be it which it may, is under discussion, it must not be supposed that it is its material composition to which attention is being directed or which is the object of discussion, but the relation of such part to the total form. . . .

As every instrument and every bodily member subserves some partial end, that is to say, some special action, so the whole body must be destined to minister to some plenary sphere of action. Thus the saw is made for sawing, for sawing is a function, and not sawing for the saw. Similarly, the body too must somehow or other be made for the soul, and each part of it for some subordinate function, to which it is adapted.[1]

To this long passage which tells us much about Aristotle's motivation and intent we must add a short one which is valuable in disclosing for us his declaration of method. It comes from a section where he is discussing the reproduction of bees:

But the facts have not yet been sufficiently ascertained; and if at any future time they are ascertained, then credence must be given to the direct evidence of the senses rather than to theories – and to theories too provided that the results which they show agree with what is observed.

Finally, let us add by way of an example of how Aristotle exemplifies his own precepts and quickens his own writing by his minute observations of nature how in observing the development of the embryo chicken he detected on the fourth day after the laying of the

[1] *Selections*, pp. 175ff.

fertilised egg the presence of the heart 'like a speck of blood in the white of the egg, beating and moving as though endowed with life'; and by way of example of how he intrigues us let us recall the case he describes of the woman of Elis who had a daughter by an Ethiopian; this daughter was not black but her son was (a phenomenon whose explanation had to await modern genetic theory).

How very different all this is from and, indeed, how very contrary to the spirit of Parmenides, Pythagoras (for the most part) and Plato's Academy. Aristotle's predilection for and bias towards biological studies would not in any sense have made it possible to predict his opposition to the static concept of Parmenides and the static Forms of Plato, but they do perhaps assist our understanding of why the central point of dissent between master and pupil was the theory of Forms; why, as F. M. Cornford put it: 'the Platonic Form of the Species is brought down from its heaven of unchanging reality, and plunged in the flow of time and sensible existence'. They help us to understand why it was Aristotle who took up Heracleitus' dynamic dictum (albeit in Professor Popper's version) 'Things are processes' and clothed it in flesh and blood. They, coupled with his genius for logic and classification, help us to understand why the species assumes such pre-eminence, and why Aristotle eternally appeals to arguments from function and teleology.

Both relatively and absolutely Aristotle was more successful in the biological field than in any other major field of enquiry. This was not because of perverseness on the part of the philosopher, although, as we shall see, he was not without some curious blind spots. It was rather that in the absence of instrumentation to facilitate experiment and more precise measurement, it was possible to make greater progress where, as Aristotle himself said 'respecting perishable plants and animals we have abundant information, living as we do in their midst, and ample data may be collected concerning all their various kinds, if only we are willing to take sufficient pains'. Indeed, Aristotle did sigh for a microscope and bemoan the fact that many terrestrial creatures which he wished to scrutinise were beneath the range of human vision. But the absence of the microscope did not hamper his work and progress here as much as the absence of a telescope hampered advance in the realm of astronomy, or as much as the lack of instruments impeded progress in other branches of physics. Also, it has been pointed out by one of the greatest authorities on Aristotle that in the physical sciences Aristotle was under greater pressure to accept the body of existing beliefs, and this presumably means those beliefs about the universe which had received the stamp of approval from Plato.

At any rate, the invention of the telescope and the work of Galileo, Kepler and Newton shattered the cosmos of Aristotle, stripped the heavenly bodies of their divinity and perfection of circular motion and superseded much of the old physical laws. And yet, there must be some oversimplification in ascribing lack of progress to the absence of techniques of instrumentation and experiment; for in the century prior to that in which Aristotle lived, had not Anaxagoras been expelled from Athens for the sin of reducing the sun to a piece of white-hot metal and the moon to a piece of incandescent rock; and had not Democritus postulated at some length a universe much more akin to ours than that which the scientific revolution of the seventeenth century destroyed?

Although Darwin paid him so well-merited and spontaneous a compliment in the words which stand at the head of this chapter, it was Darwin who fixed the final and perhaps the widest gulf between us and Aristotle. To Darwin we might add what Tennyson called the 'terrible Muses' Astronomy and Geology; 'terrible' because of the vistas and the magnitude of change which they opened up to human vision. Aristotle was fundamentally and consciously anti-evolutionary. This may seem paradoxical since we have considered Aristotle primarily as an exponent of movement, change and development, and that within the realm of natural history in particular. But in spite of his preoccupation with the eternal rhythm of 'potential' into 'actual', in spite of his awareness of a 'scale of Nature' stretching from lower to higher forms of life, Aristotle could only conceive of and would only admit change and motion within a certain limited frame. Acorn 'moved' into oak, egg 'moved' into hen, boy 'moved' into man; there was cyclic movement within the species just as there was circular movement in the heavens. But the species themselves like the paths of the celestial bodies, indeed, like Plato's Forms, were fixed, finite and eternal. Aristotle the biologist was perfectly at home with the flux of Nature just as Aristotle the physicist was unperturbed by the change and motion of celestial and terrestrial substances. But had he discovered there was a time when, for example, horses were no larger than greyhounds and had anatomical features very different from Bucephalus, had he discovered indeed that there was a time in the earth's history when there was no horse at all, had he discovered that the moon might conceivably have spiralled off the body of the earth and might as conceivably spiral 'down' again, had he discovered the possibility of the sun changing its mass or temperature, in other words had he found his fixed frame of reference to be subject to shift his whole philosophic structure would have received as damaging a blow as did that of the Pythagoreans when the discovery was made that number could be irrational.

It might be well perhaps to emphasise at this point that it is not a matter of taxing Aristotle with ignorance of a scientific theory with which we have only become familiar in the nineteenth and twentieth centuries. What is relevant to our study at this point is to know that where his predecessors indicated – however tentatively – pointers towards an evolutionary explanation of things, Aristotle was in no uncertain disagreement and 'corrected' them. For example, in discussing the fact that in man the forelegs and forefeet are replaced by arms and hands Aristotle takes the point of view that man stands upright because of his more god-like nature and essence in comparison with other animals, not that he has the superior quality because he stands upright. He writes:

> Now it is the opinion of Anaxagoras that the possession of these hands is the cause of man being of all animals the most intelligent. But it is more rational to suppose that his endowment with hands is the consequence rather than the cause of his superior intelligence. For the hands are instruments or organs, and the invariable plan of nature in distributing the organs is to give each to such animal as can make use of it; nature acting in this matter as any prudent man would do. For it is a better plan to take a person who is already a flute-player and give him a flute, than to take one who possesses a flute and teach him the art of flute-playing.[1]

We find a similar argument in *The Politics* in the consideration of man and speech:

> ... for obviously man is a political animal in a sense in which a bee is not, or any gregarious animal. Nature, as we say, does nothing without some purpose; and for the purpose of making man a political animal she has endowed him alone among the animals with the power of reasoned speech.[2]

GP M   [1] Ibid., p. 182.   [2] p. 28 (Penguin).

Aristotle believes profoundly that Nature is like a good housewife who has the contents of her rooms arranged in a functional way and according to a plan; he takes Democritus to task for proposing that the heavens (of all things for Aristotle the most orderly) might be constructed by a haphazard confluence of atoms, and he argues against Empedocles who propounded the theory that new creatures could arise by the chance growth of new limbs or by new arrangements of limbs. To argue as Empedocles and Democritus do would involve the throwing overboard of both formal and final Causes and this Aristotle obviously could not allow. It is not only the idea of chance and the haphazard in the two former philosophers which should be here noted but the idea of flexibility, a flexibility which left their scheme of things open to improvement as man's knowledge of the universe advanced. For all the mobility within it, Aristotle's cosmos was too rigid, too cut and dried with every pocket of it too neatly labelled. If it did not prove to be in accord with the later inflow of knowledge, it could not survive.

What a man chooses to believe depends upon factors very much more complex and more deeply concealed than the sum total of facts at his disposal. We find striking examples of this in Aristotle's attitude to slavery, to non-Greeks and to the historical institution of the city state as he reveals it to us in *The Politics*.

Leaning heavily on analogies from the biological field Aristotle argues that it is in accordance with the LAW OF NATURE that not only should man rule woman and Greek rule non-Greek, but that just as soul rules body, free men should rule slaves. We should note the wording carefully when he writes:

> It is then part of nature's intention to make the bodies of free men to differ from those of slaves, the latter strong enough for the necessary menial tasks, the former erect and useless for that kind of work, but well suited for the life of a citizen of a state, a life divided between war and peace.[1]

When he proceeds to indicate the source from which these slaves may be drawn, Aristotle uses words which, coming from the mind responsible for *The Organon*, makes us look with near incredulity:

> If then we are right in believing that nature makes nothing without some end in view, nothing to no purpose, it must be that

[1] Ibid., p. 34.

nature has made all things specifically for the sake of man. This means that it is part of nature's plan that the art of war, of which hunting is a part, should be a way of acquiring property (in this case, slaves); and that it must be used both against wild beasts and *against such men as are by nature intended to be ruled over but refuse.*[1]

We would mislead ourselves if we were to imagine that the institution of slavery was not in question at this time and that Aristotle was merely accepting a state of affairs which was, in the Greek world at any rate, universally acceptable. He explains that there were those who held that slavery might indeed be expedient, but was certainly not right, was certainly a convention, and so was not necessitated by any law of Nature.

Again, not only do there appear to have been fundamental differences between Alexander and his former tutor about the most appropriate way to treat the Asiatic peoples who came under the former's domination, but the philosopher appears to have turned a blind eye to the ecumenical movement initiated by the Macedonian army and its leader and to have written about the city state in a parochial way as though no such momentous change were taking place.

How then does it come about that one who has so deep a knowledge of his fellow men, who showed at death a kindly and generous disposition towards his slaves and who was endowed with such outstanding intellectual power should have so distorted reason here? We have seen in *The Ethics* and *The Politics* that the supreme end for man was to be as like God as possible, i.e. to engage in pure contemplation, and that leisure and philosophy were prerequisites of this activity. An adequate supply of slaves was, in turn, the prerequisite of a body of citizens sufficiently provided with the necessities of life and leisure to philosophise. Put very briefly, the salvation of some and the very existence of philosophy depended on the enslavement of others. Aristotle does hint at a way out of this dilemma. It is the mere product of fancy, and all the more so in that at this time in Athenian society the divorce between those who pursued philosophy and those who were engaged in manual or technical tasks was complete, and yet it comes at the beginning of Aristotle's exposition on the subject of slavery, in the first book of *The Politics*. He writes:

[1] Ibid., p. 40.

For suppose that every tool we had could perform its function, either at our bidding or itself perceiving the need, . . . and suppose that shuttles in a loom could fly to and fro and a plucker play on a lyre all self-moved, *then manufacturers would have no need of workers nor masters of slaves.*[1]

It is often asked why this mechanical solution totally eluded the Greeks who are so constantly portrayed as a race of rare intellectual acumen. Historical questions of this sort are difficult to answer satisfactorily, and particularly for a period for which statistical information is so scanty. At any rate, in the absence of the automatic shuttle and in the interests of knowledge Socrates is said to have mortified the body and even at the end to have courted its destruction; Diogenes lived in his barrel with humble begging-bowl; but Aristotle kept his slaves for he is reputed to have liked good clothes!

We have said much about Aristotle in relation to his predecessors and his own times; what of his reputation in subsequent centuries? During the Middle Ages until about the year 1200 only his works on Logic were known and studied in Christian Europe. From that date onward translations from the Arab world began to flow into the medieval universities. The interesting effect is described by F. C. Copleston:

When the Corpus Aristotelicum was made known to medieval Christendom, a new world was opened to men's minds. For here was a wealth of observation, reflection and theory which was new to the medieval. It came with the charm of novelty and it was impressed with the stamp of an outstanding thinker: it offered an interpretation of reality which far exceeded in its richness and comprehensiveness anything which the medieval philosophers had yet provided. Thus if one tries to put oneself in the place of a university student in the early part of the thirteenth century, it is not difficult to understand the interest and enthusiasm which Aristotle aroused. For many people today Aristotelianism is something old and obsolete; but for the student of whom I am speaking it was like a new revelation, throwing a fresh light on the world. Moreover, since it was obvious that Aristotelianism stood, as it were, on its own feet and owed nothing to Christianity, men's ideas of the nature and scope of philosophy were necessarily enlarged.[2]

---

[1] Ibid., p. 31.
[2] *Aquinas*, p. 61 (Penguin).

Indeed – for such are the changes of doctrinal climate – this Aristotelian philosophy was more than merely 'new'; it was dangerous, and for a time was subject to papal interdiction. This is hardly surprising when we recollect that in Aristotle we found no personal God, no creation and – in spite of a little equivocation – no personal immortality. But before the thirteenth century was out he had become for Aquinas 'the philosopher' and for Dante 'the master of those that know'. Much of Chaucer, Shakespeare and Milton loses force for those unacquainted to some degree with Aristotle's universe. As Donne wrote in one of his Devotions: 'Young men mend not their sight by using old men's spectacles, and yet we looke upon Nature but with Aristotle's spectacles. . . .'

Since the seventeenth century all is changed. 'Ever since the beginning of the seventeenth century,' writes Bertrand Russell, 'almost every serious intellectual advance has had to begin with an attack on some Aristotelian doctrine; in Logic this is still true at the present day. But it would have been at least as disastrous if any of his predecessors (except perhaps Democritus) had acquired equal authority. To do him justice, we must, to begin with, forget his excessive posthumous fame, and the equally excessive posthumous condemnation to which it led.'[1]

[1] *History of Western Philosophy*, p. 173 (Allen and Unwin).

CHAPTER XIX

Hellenism and Alexandria

Athens is not the sea power of our fathers but
a gruel-guzzling old slattern in slippers.

A HELLENISTIC POET

No honest man I call a foreigner;
One nature have we all.

MENANDER

The mind is its own place, and in itself
Can make a heaven of hell, a hell of heaven.

JOHN MILTON

'I am Alexander, the King.'
      'I am Diogenes, the dog.'
      'Are you afraid of me?'
   'Why, what are you, a good thing, or a bad?'
   'Good.'
   'Who's afraid of the good?'
   'Ask anything you like of me.'
   'Don't keep the sun off me.'
   'If I were not Alexander, I should wish to be Diogenes.'
   The setting of this familiar, if fictitious, dialogue was the city of
Corinth, where a conference of the city states of Greece – auto-
nomous no more – acknowledged Alexander as their head. Un-
willingly they acquiesced in what the Macedonian phalanx had made
it useless to oppose. In this little scene we have the twin features of
the new, the Hellenistic or Alexandrian age.
   Alexander the king, having put an end to the period we know as
Classical, was about to sweep like a mighty solvent from the Aegean
to the Indus, loosening the old political ties, shaking up existing
social institutions. The new era which began with Alexander's death

in 323 B.C. was brought to its close in 30 B.C. by the death of Mark Antony. Far truer was it of Alexander than of Antony that

> . . . in his livery
> Walked crowns and coronets; realms and
>   islands were
> As plates dropped from his pocket.

Peculiarly characteristic of Alexander was the legend of the Gordian knot. Tucked away in the Phrygian village of Gordium was a waggon dedicated many centuries before to Zeus. The yoke was fastened to the waggon with a secret knot and it was decreed by fate that he who opened this knot would master Asia. Alexander, a king, not a philosopher, severed the knot in a twinkling with his sword. Not for him the doctrine that the seeker after truth 'about it and about must go'. Philosophers such as Socrates, Plato and Aristotle were all long-lived; Alexander, moving on from Gordium, mastered Asia and died when thirty-three.

Diogenes, the dog, withdrawn from the world, was tied to his tub and his pathetic little begging-bowl. He asked of life as little as possible but was determined that if all else had become the personal property of those who possessed the means to pay, the sunlight was his as much as Alexander's.

The process of withdrawal had been begun by Socrates who admitted that had he taken an active part in the affairs of Athens his life would have ended earlier than it did. Plato and Aristotle withdrew to the extent that they spent their lives – apart from certain brief and unsuccessful interludes – in their secluded groves teaching political ideals to others. One is very close to 'the hushed cult of Beauty' and 'the fugitive and cloistered virtue' in Plato's dialogues. Plato sailed twice to Sicily to accept, albeit reluctantly, a challenge to mould the young ruler of Syracuse into a philosopher-king; for as Plutarch pointed out, he did not wish to appear that he was 'all theory'. But Dionysius, prince of Syracuse, proved no more influenced by Plato's mathematics than, in later years, was Alexander by Aristotle's politics.

Antisthenes, a pupil and friend of Socrates, had founded the School of Cynics to which Diogenes was the most spectacular adherent. Antisthenes, following the characteristic pattern of the nobly born who espouse a life of simple saintliness, renouncing his wealth and circle of aristocrats, adopted a humble anarchistic attitude and cultivated the friendship of working men and slaves. His flagrant flouting of the established conventions of his time was his protest against their sham and hollowness. He found an unusual degree of support from Diogenes, a wandering exile who, on asking the oracle at Delphi what he must do to become famous, was advised 'to cheat the Customs'. (The characteristic oracular *double entendre* lay here in the Greek word *nomismata* which could mean customs, conventions or coinage.) So Diogenes defied conventions and played the dog by repudiating this world's goods and proclaiming the brotherhood of man and the virtues of freedom from desires. The name Cynic means 'dog-man'. A. H. Armstrong explains:

> The dog for the Greeks was the type of shamelessness, and a short meditation on the things dogs do in public will show the direction which Cynic flouting of convention took. Diogenes in particular carried this to extremes.[1]

But Diogenes' drab tub is an important symbol of the changes which were taking place in the Greek world. Compare the condition of its tenant with the dignity of a Sophocles or the confidence of a Pericles, and it is clear that history has been moving rapidly. The city states, which had, as it were, mothered their citizens, were breaking up and this was causing widespread insecurity and fear. In Athens, for example, Athene no longer presided over her own; the presidency had moved to Macedon, cold, remorseless and remote; and citizens who once by corporate courage and conviction directed actively their own fate at every turn were now reduced to helpless, passive ciphers. The ferment Plato feared was permeating the whole of Alexander's empire. The conqueror himself was smashing convention on an unprecedented scale; marrying oriental wives, mingling Greek with barbarian, worshipping strange gods. His conquest set up mighty economic movements whose wash was felt all round the Aegean shores. As the rich increased their wealth and the poor sank deeper into misery and debt, that healthy middle class on which Aristotle had relied for moderation and stability disintegrated. With the security of community life now gone, the individual found himself adrift on a political and economic ocean which was unfamiliar and uncharted. It was in answer to distress signals, sent out

---

[1] *An Introduction to Ancient Philosophy*, p. 118 (Methuen).

by men in such a situation, that the new philosophies of the Hellenistic world appeared.

Of these the most important were Stoicism – into which the Cynics gradually merged – and Epicureanism, founded almost simultaneously in Athens. Although these two had common aims – the rescue of the individual – some of their fundamental tenets differed widely. Philosophy no longer sought to explain 'just causes' or the 'nature of reality'. It no longer dared attempt to construct Utopias. Heaven and earth had suffered upheavals too great. The questions now demanding instant answer were: How can man be virtuous in a shifting, shifty world? How can man find happiness in the midst of universal and relentless suffering?

In 315 B.C. Zeno, a Phoenician businessman from Cyprus, bought up or rented in the market place of Athens a Stoa or Colonnade which was adorned with frescoes by some of the city's outstanding painters and which was a favourite meeting place for citizens. It may be significant that Zeno selected no secluded grove or haunt of Muses.

The philosophy which Zeno propounded to those who thronged his painted colonnade – and who were therefore called the Stoics – reflected the kind of world which Alexander had created. It embraced the opposing ideas of cosmopolitanism and individualism. Since, in a world ruled by indiscriminating Chance, attachments were inevitably accompanied by disappointment and sorrow, men must prune their worldly pleasures to the minimum, so that when Chance does strike they will be found to be both 'self-sufficient' and unperturbed. The material world was real, horribly real; it could not be ignored by calling it an illusion of the senses as Plato and Parmenides had done. Rather it must be matched by individual will and courage such as were displayed by Socrates. The dominion of the city states was now expanded and in the hands of dynastics. The dominion over which a citizen had control had been contracted to the area of his own heart and mind; but there at any rate he could be master.

But this principle of imperturbable self-sufficiency which Zeno learned to practise from his friends Antisthenes and Diogenes was little more than practical advice. Ethics alone which have no roots in a supporting creed are weak and wither easily for lack of nourishment. Drawing upon the doctrines of Anaximenes and Heracleitus, the creed which Zeno used to clothe his Ethics was briefly this. Pervading all the universe is an Immanent Will which may be thought of variously as Fiery Breath, a Principle of Reason or God. This Fiery Breath is in all things and gives life and value to the otherwise insipid framework of the universe 'like honey in the honeycomb'. Conversely all life returns from time to time in periodic conflagrations to Fire, its creator, and cycle follows cycle each one reproducing a pattern of the world identical with its predecessor. All nature moves in accordance with this vital principle manifested as Reason; to live in accordance with this Reason must be man's aim. There is a guiding Providence working through our apparently disordered world. Since all men were animated by a portion of the Divine Breath all men were ennobled and members of one family.

Stoic doctrine strikes the modern reader as being curiously ill-defined and contradictory. But then the *oekumene* or inhabited world which it reflected was likewise lacking in delineation, and inconsistent. To Zeno, of oriental origin, now domiciled in Greece, what more natural than that he who held all things in his hand, the king of kings, should have appeared as a fiery breath, a 'meteor with beard of flame' fusing the peoples of Asia into one brotherhood? Just as Heracleitus explained that his fire was like Phoenician currency of the time – it could be exchanged for anything – so Alexander's energy could appear in different forms: fiery breath, will, reason, providence.

It is interesting that the philosophy of the Painted Porch arising in the world of Alexander was reinforced at Rome in the principate of Augustus Caesar and his successors. The Pax Romana of Augustus took over the task which Macedon began. The basic articles of the Stoic creed, which thus enjoyed no mean longevity, were subject to constant modifications and accretions. It undeniably assisted man to retain nobility and dignity under the greatest excesses of the Roman emperors. Its primary weakness was its inability to exclude the cheap astrology and superstition which spread from Babylonia westward like a philosophy-engulfing flood in Hellenistic times. In the course of its development from Zeno to the Roman, Marcus Aurelius, Stoicism turned away from the materialist outlook of its early impulse, became confused with Platonism and, particularly in Rome, appealed to ruling circles.

Epicurus, another voluminous writer whose works, some hundreds, have not survived, provided an alternative refuge for the troubled Hellenistic age. It is all too easy with the English 'Epicurean' in our minds to form an image of a Greek who taught and practised a kind of fastidious hedonism. Our image might seem further justified on finding that the oft quoted maxim 'Pleasure is the beginning and end of the blessed life' is ascribed to this philosopher.

Born on the island of Samos of Athenian parents, Epicurus founded a community in a house and surrounding precincts in Athens. His School is frequently referred to as 'the Garden'. Here he taught his followers to achieve tranquillity. From an inscription on the cloisters of a similar Epicurean community in a town in Asia Minor we can see the kernel of their ethical belief. The inscription ran: 'Nothing to fear in God. Nothing to feel in Death. Good can be attained. Evil can be endured.' Epicurus was convinced that apart from physical pain – he himself was afflicted much by a chronic illness – men suffered most from fear: fear of religion and the sanctions it ordained, and fear of death. All religion and philosophy associated with Orpheus, Pythagoras and Plato inculcated fear of punishment after death and the possibility of eternal torment for the separable soul. Such systems not only filled the mind with dread but furnished the 'Guardians' of the state with a convenient curb to bridle any men of 'brass' who might prove recalcitrant. That the widespread, popular cult of paternal and punitive godhead had been encouraged as an instrument of government had been suggested by a number of authors of antiquity, not least among whom was Plato's notorious relative Critias.

It is interesting that just about the time that Epicurus arrived in Athens and upon the retirement of Macedon's regent from the city, an upsurge of democratic feeling and legal action was directed against the Schools of Plato and Aristotle (now, of course, in the hands of their successors). Had not Plato's friends been notoriously inimical to the democracy? Had not Aristotle been under the protection of the domineering Macedonian dynasty? The upshot of the legal process was that since both the Academy and Lyceum were registered as religious societies sacred to the Muses, it was against Athenian law for them to be disturbed and the citizen who brought the action was expelled. As Epicurus was quick to see, the weighty and influential political teaching carried on in both secluded groves was uniformly aristocratic and enjoyed immunity under the name of religion.

Epicurus, trained in the school of Democritus, described in Chapter IX, accepted and slightly modified the atomic theory of the universe on which to base his Ethics. The universe and all within it were composed of atoms and void. Body, Soul and Mind had a material basis. Knowledge, wisdom and memory resulted from the impact, through the channels of the senses, of stimuli from without upon material soul within. Knowledge so acquired was real. Had not Democritus clearly warned the Idealists when he made the senses speak to the Intellect thus: 'Miserable mind, you get your evidence from us and do you try to overthrow us? The overthrow will be your downfall.'?

For Epicurus the gods existed but they existed out in the intermundane spaces, heedless of the affairs of men. At death the atoms of the human soul were subject to dissolution and rearrangement: no aggregate of atoms comprising personal soul survived the blow of death. By reason of the indeterminate swerve on the part of atoms man was endowed with freedom of the will. Men who believe the universe to be infinite and their own world to be one of many similar do not readily fall prey to the insidious superstition and astrology which the Academy and later Stoa all too readily embraced. (The distinction between mathematical symbolism and the Cabal is very fine.)

Armed with a doctrine of physics such as this, Epicurus devoted his life to 'bringing soothing solace to the minds of men'. For some four centuries The Garden and The Stoa stood as philosophic rivals and The Stoa, backed by administrative power, won. But the efficacy of Epicurus' ethic, at any rate for those within the orbit of his School, is gratefully commemorated by Lucretius' lines: 'When human life lay grovelling in all men's sight, crushed to the earth under the dead weight of superstition whose grim features loomed menacingly upon mortals from the four quarters of the sky, a man from Greece was first to raise mortal eyes in defiance, first to stand erect and brave the challenge. Fables of the gods did not crush him, nor the lightning flash and the growling menace of the sky. . . . Therefore superstition in its turn lies crushed beneath his feet, and we by his triumph are lifted level with the skies.'[1]

---

[1] *The Nature of the Universe*, p. 29 (Penguin).

Paradoxically while philosophic man withdrew in Stoic fortitude or Epicurean calm, explorer and merchant ventured outward to chart unfamiliar seas and coastlines. Just as holy Olympia had once been the focal point for the reunion of the Greek race from Eastern and Western Europe, so now cosmopolitan Alexandria was the centre where men assembled to exchange goods, gods and navigation aids from places as widely distant as the Punjab and Cadiz. It is not surprising that such activity was accompanied by a great upsurge of interest and success in the sciences which map and measure heavens, seas and earth.

Quickly responding to the temper of the times the first members of the Ptolemaic dynasty founded in Alexandria the Library and the Museum. These formed a vast repository and clearing house for rapidly accumulating knowledge in the spheres of literature, mathematics, astronomy and medicine (of which natural history was a part). Scholars of international repute met there and learning flourished. The old Milesian times of Thales were reborn and on a vaster scale. Observation was the key to knowledge once again and men looked outwards with fresh and uninhibited eyes.

Philosophy remained in Athens and the division of philosophy from observational science insisted on by Socrates and Plato was complete. Aristotle, colossus that he was, bestrode the gap between Athens and Alexandria. For how better could the new empiric methods have been introduced to the Museum's department of Medicine and Natural History than through Aristotle's work? Where better could the Alexandrian literary critics begin than with his *Rhetoric* and *Poetics*? And more than that. The first head of the Lyceum had taught his pupils once that not only was the earth a sphere but that the distance between Spain and India by way of the Atlantic Ocean might not be very great.

It was Eratosthenes in Alexandria who not only confirmed for all the earth's sphericity but measured the equator's length by a neat experiment based on observation. It was Eratosthenes who popularised for Europe the idea, first proposed by Aristotle, which sent Columbus sailing westward.

By none is the visual and intellectual acuity of these men better demonstrated than by Aristarchus of Samos who, says Archimedes, 'brought out a book consisting of some hypotheses, wherein it appears, from the assumptions made, that the universe is many

GP N

times larger than the universe as commonly understood by astronomers, his hypothesis being "*That the fixed stars and the sun remain unmoved, and the earth revolves about the sun in the circumference of a circle . . .*"'

However, such a theory would have robbed the universe of its absolute centre and men of their confidence that astrological and providential beams were playing on their earth; it would have robbed many of their teleology and would have made the Hellenistic age, confounded fearfully on earth, confounded worse in heaven. So Cleanthes, now head of the Stoic world, proposed that Aristarchus be indicted on a charge of blasphemy.

Suggested Reading

Bevan, Edwyn. *Stoics and Sceptics* (Oxford).
Sambursky, S. *Physics of the Stoics* (Routledge).
Tarn, W. W., and Others. *The Hellenistic Age* (Cambridge).

CHAPTER XX

Conclusion

The Dichotomies – The Convergence of the Twain

> Then felt I like some watcher of the skies
> When a new planet swims into his ken;
> Or like stout Cortez when with eagle eyes
> He stared at the Pacific – and all his men
> Looked at each other with a wild surmise –
> Silent, upon a peak in Darien.[1]

Yet the author was exploring neither the geographical world nor the heavens. He was merely reading a book; a new translation of an ancient poet – Homer. Complementary to this we have such a statement as that of Sartre when he says: 'Saint Exupéry has shown us that, for the pilot, the aeroplane is an organ of perception.' So that what the printed page did for one, a product of science and technology did for the other. Each in his own way was increasing his knowledge of the universe, each in his own way was nourishing and enlarging his imaginative experience. Estrangement between art on the one hand and science and technology on the other need be neither inevitable nor permanent.

But there is a further cleavage: the cleavage between the pursuit of pure mathematics and science and the applied sciences, including anything which smacks of technology. In an age such as ours with its unparalleled demand for men and women who can apply mathematics to almost every field of modern life, with its constant cry for mathematics to assist in every kind of engineering, industrial and social expansion, it is surprising to find the cleavage so persistent. And yet so widespread is it that one reads today: '. . . the supply [of industrial mathematicians] is inadequate, and inappropriately trained. Indeed it has been said that "the value of a mathematician

[1] Keats: *On First Looking into Chapman's Homer.*

to industry is inversely proportional to the quality of his degree" '.
This, of course, is a direct descendant of the celebrated toast: 'Here's
to mathematics and may it never be any use!'

Now these dichotomies are more fundamental and have roots
stretching further back into the past than is often realised. We have
seen that early Greek thought was as much physics as it was philosophy; that with Socrates a 'separating out' process appeared; that
Plato and Aristotle emphasised the pejorative sense of the word
'banausic'; and that with the establishing of the Museum in Alexandria, science and philosophy agreed to remain separate. On
looking back we feel that Plato is rather like a man who would scorn
newly-discovered electric light because the water turning the
generating turbine was impure; Aristotle like one who would use
the light for midnight toil as long as the turbine was neither turned
nor tended by fully enfranchised citizens; Thales and Empedocles
would have enjoyed the light, incorporated the significance of
electricity and magnetism into their philosophy and invented an
improved version of the generating plant.

We have seen that with the decline of the city state Philosophy
turned away from the study of the properties of matter. Along with
this decline – whether as cause or effect is not here the point – went
an increase in the influx of slaves and non-citizen artisans to Athens.
This greater dependence on slave and resident-alien labour was a
potent factor not only in the trend towards philosophic Idealism and
a more rarefied kind of theorising, but also in the arresting of Greek
science and technology, so that when, as late as the second century
A.D., a person like Hero of Alexandria showed considerable knowledge of the physics of power, that knowledge was applied to
nothing more than a few 'gimmicks': a coin-in-the-slot juke box,
an automatic holy water dispenser and a small body made to rotate
by the action of jets of expanding air – rather like a chicken on a spit.

To assign such an arresting role to the institution of Greek slavery
is, of course, something of an oversimplification of a movement
which was highly complex. The full story would need a separate
study and social statistics which scarcely exist. We may recall in this
context the words of A. N. Whitehead in *Science and the Modern
World*: 'The reason why we are on a higher imaginative level is not
because we have finer imaginations, but because we have better
instruments.' And we might well say that one important reason for

the Greeks' lack of better instruments was their difficulty in producing iron and steel in sufficiently large quantities and with the required carbon content. There may well, too, have been psychological reasons caused by the passing away of the comparative security, cohesion and personal involvement associated with city state conditions. Nevertheless, it is relevant to say something further about the effects of slavery.

It is axiomatic amongst empiricists that Fortune favours the prepared mind. Any sop, however tiny, thrown by Fortune in the path of an experimentalist's mind which is on the alert is quickly snapped up and assimilated into valuable growth. Any scientist, moreover, could enlarge upon the theme that very many discoveries, some trivial, some important, from teepol to penicillin, are accidental or part accidental. But in such cases the accident always happens in the vicinity of trained minds. In Greece from about the time of Socrates onwards trained minds were seldom, if ever, in contact with practical processes. However magnanimous and considerate Aristotle was towards his own slaves, as long as they were the accepted labour force of society, the master could not be seen associating with work which could only properly be done by them, and he was therefore most unlikely to invent a 'shuttle that could weave without a hand to guide it'. Indeed, if society had demanded that men of the calibre of Aristotle and Archimedes should weave their own shirts, the first automatic shuttle might well have been located in Athens or Syracuse. The invention of an automatic, mechanically efficient shuttle would not have been so very difficult for a man who had exclaimed, as had Archimedes, that if he had a fulcrum, a lever long enough and somewhere to stand, he could shift the world.

In 212 B.C. when the Roman general Marcellus was besieging Syracuse, its ruler Hiero requested Archimedes to translate his mathematics into practical terms which might be appreciated by the people and might assist the city in its need. The result was a battery of machines which played havoc with the Roman fleet. (Earlier, in time of peace, Archimedes had demonstrated to the citizens his system of pulleys by hauling single handed a fully laden galley along the shore.) Plutarch, explaining why this kind of thing was distasteful to Archimedes and carried out under some degree of protest, writes:

But what with Plato's indignation at it [i.e. the application of mathematics in this way], and his invectives against it as the mere corruption and annihilation of the one good of geometry which was thus shamefully turning its back upon the unembodied objects of pure intelligence to have recourse to sensation, and to ask help from matter; so it was that mechanics came to be separated from geometry, and, repudiated and neglected by philosophers, took its place as a military art. . . . But, [Archimedes] repudiating as sordid and ignoble the whole trade of engineering and every sort of art that lends itself to mere use and profit, he placed his whole affection and ambition in those purer speculations where there can be no reference to the vulgar needs of life.[1]

This, of course, stems from the discussion on mathematical training in *The Republic* where Socrates says firmly that there will be no mathematical practices and no terminology which are in any way 'redolent of the workshop'.

Dichotomies – partly because they represent a kind of blindness – can be dangerous. With administrators excluded from a ready understanding of the secrets of nature and with scientists deprived of a deep understanding of humanism and historical perspective, scientific advance and the demands it makes could become a destroying, dehumanising monster. It is not without reason that from time to time leading men of letters feel compelled to diminish the stature of contemporary scientific culture. William Blake was an outstanding example of the artist striving to reclaim for man an ampler spiritual life and imagination as opposed to the calculations of the scientist and the spreading squalor of technologist and industrialist:

> I turn my eyes to the Schools and Universities of Europe,
> And there behold the Loom of Locke, whose woof rages
> > dire,
> Wash'd by the Water-wheels of Newton: black the cloth
> In heavy wreath folds over every Nation: cruel Works
> Of many wheels I view, wheel without wheel, with
> > cogs tyrannic,
> Moving by compulsion each other; not as those in
> > Eden, which,
> Wheel within wheel, in freedom revolve, in harmony
> > and peace.[2]

[1] *Life of Marcellus* (Everyman's Library, Dent).
[2] *Selections from Jerusalem* (Oxford).

And:

> Thus the terrible race of Los and Enitharmon gave
> Laws and Religions to the sons of Har, binding them
> more
> And more to Earth, closing and restraining;
> Till a Philosophy of Five Senses was complete:
> Urizen wept, and gave it into the hands of Newton
> and Locke.[1]

And again:

> The Atoms of Democritus
> And Newton's particles of light
> Are sands upon the Red Sea Shore
> Where Israel's tents do shine so bright.[2]

Urizen may mean 'the Setter of Boundaries' or 'Your Reason'. In either case he aroused the wrath of Blake who felt that, spiritually and imaginatively speaking, nothing short of the infinite was good enough for man. Newton had, of course, continued the line of atomic thought set off by Democritus, and Israel's tents here represent the spiritual life as opposed to mechanistic and materialistic modes of thought.

It is interesting that Blake and Epicurus were at one in wanting an end to the restrictive practices of contemporary priests and in seeking to create an atmosphere of freedom and joy for their fellow men. Yet for Epicurus the denigration of the senses was associated with the wielding of superstition and ignorance as an instrument of tyranny, while for Blake the scientists – champions of the five senses – were the creators of sorrow, wheels and 'cogs tyrannic', the destroyers of spiritual and artistic imagination. If science were to become soulless, devoid of wonder and imagination, distorted in purpose and in presentation, society would have to adopt once more the attitude of Blake. Many would assert that such a point has already been reached; others see more hope.

Jowett, in his commentary on Plato's dialogue, *The Theaetetus*, said, 'The writings of Plato belong to an age in which the power of analysis has outrun the means of knowledge.' Today the knowledge and the means of knowledge multiply at an exciting if bewildering pace. Philosophy and art have ample opportunity to revert to what

---

[1] *The Song of Los.*   [2] *Poems from the Rossetti MS.*

was once their role; that of tribunal sifting the evidence piling up before it, working upon it and presenting it in order. It was in this same dialogue that Plato gave a clue towards the role of philosophy (and we might add art) when he said, 'The sense of wonder is characteristic of a philosopher; wonder, in fact, is the very source of speculation, and he who made Iris (the Rainbow) the daughter of Thaumas (Wonder) was a good genealogist.' It is surely neither too fanciful nor too extravagant to claim that science today is producing not only the material for both philosophy and art to work on, but also the Wonder. And, after all, could anything bridge a gap more beautifully than a rainbow?

The conflict between the 'banausic' and more gentlemanly pursuits does not stem merely from the time and writings of Plato and Aristotle. The banausic, in the shape of foundry, forge or furnace, had figured in an earlier conflict in the folk-consciousness of the Greeks: in the conflict between Prometheus, the Titan (in part identified with Hephaestus, the god of the smithy) and Zeus, ruler of Olympus. Prometheus, according to mythology, created man from clay and, in the face of opposition from Zeus, brought down fire from heaven and taught his creation the uses of it. For giving man this power, Zeus had the Titan chained to a Caucasian rock to suffer torment. Hephaestus too, whose forge may be identified with the source of the offending fire – normally reserved for forging the weapons for the punitive hand of Zeus – not only fell out of favour in Olympus but was hurled out of heaven.

Can one discern a pattern in life from Prometheus to the present day; a pattern of conflict – whether in heaven or on earth – between Scientist and Guardian, between scientific knowledge and Guardian-Art?

The Greeks knew that man was a potential Titan. They said so in their drama. They knew, too, that there was a terrible attendant risk, for man's creative was equalled only by his destructive and more particularly his self-destructive power. This risk was chiefly psychological and was a constant theme of Athenian Tragedy. Others, notably Parmenides, Empedocles, the atomists and Aristotle had written about psychology from the point of view of the physiology or the validity of sense perception. But it was the dramatists who studied deeply and portrayed with insight the reactions of the human mind in the course of man's dealings with Fate. It was they

who, in play after play, tried to bring home to their city the inexorable course of the Tragic Sequence – inexorable at any rate after
a certain point. Although the study of Tragedy does not properly
fall within the limits of philosophy, the psychology involved in the
working of this Tragic Sequence is a most important part of Greek
thought. There were five stages in this sequence:

1. *Olbos* : worldly happiness, wealth.
2. *Koros* : surfeit, the mother of Hubris.
3. *Hubris* : wanton violence arising from *pride* in strength.
4. *Peitho* : persuasion (to perform the deed which leads to the
final tragedy).
5. *Ate* : ruin, destruction.

There was a psychological antidote. It was the possession of a
quality of mind revered by the Greeks both in private and public life
and in their art: the quality of *aidos*, or modesty and reserve in the
midst of and in spite of power and success. A well known exemplar
of the quality of *aidos* is the bronze statue of the victorious charioteer
which stands in Delphi. There are some who detect the faintest
flicker of a smile in one corner of the young man's mouth: *aidos* is
present but the victor is human. This, surely, is one of the most
beautiful and adult of the conceptions which have come down to us
from the Greeks. If the Athenians, who had Hubris so constantly
before their minds, from time to time fell a prey to it, how much
more likely and with what more terrible consequences might a
scientific age do the same? Dichotomies may bring about two kinds
of convergence: convergence through understanding with *aidos*
present, or the kind of convergence of Thomas Hardy's remarkable
poem *The Convergence of the Twain*:

> In a solitude of the sea
> Deep from human vanity,
> And the Pride of Life that planned her, stilly couches she.
>
> Steel chambers, late the pyres
> Of her salamandrine fires,
> Cold currents thrid, and turn to rhythmic tidal lyres.
>
> Over the mirrors meant
> To glass the opulent
> The sea-worm crawls – grotesque, slimed, dumb, indifferent.

Jewels in joy designed
To ravish the sensuous mind
Lie lightless, all their sparkles bleared and black and blind.

Dim moon-eyed fishes near
Gaze at the gilded gear
And query: 'What does this vaingloriousness down here?'

Well: while was fashioning
This creature of cleaving wing,
The Imminent Will that stirs and urges everything

Prepared a sinister mate
For her – so gaily great –
A Shape of Ice, for the time far and dissociate.

And as the smart ship grew
In stature, grace, and hue
In shadowy silent distance grew the Iceberg too.

Alien they seemed to be:
No mortal eye could see
The intimate welding of their history,

Or sign that they were bent
By paths coincident
On being anon twin halves of one august event.

Till the Spinner of the years
Said 'NOW!' And each one hears,
And consummation comes, and jars two hemispheres.[1]

SUGGESTED READING

Hull, L. W. H. *History and Philosophy of Science* (Longmans).

[1] *Collected Poems* (Macmillan).

Index

Academy, Plato's, 48, 90, 115, 123, 130, 133-4, 152, 165, 177-8
Acoustics, 28, 35
Actual, 49, 141-2, 147, 166
Aeschylus, 58
Aidos (Modesty), 187
Air (Mist), 20-24, 37-38, 52-54, 57, 101, 145-6
Aither (Aether), 23, 146
Alcmaeon of Croton, 138
Alexander the Great, 133, 169, 172 ff.
Alexandria, 179
   Museum of, 62, 179, 182
Amber, Baltic, 19
Analytics, Prior and *Posterior*, 135; *Prior*, 137
Anamnesis (Recollection), 94, 99, 125, 126
Anaxagoras, 1, 58 ff., 65, 66, 68, 85, 166, 167
Anaximander, 19 ff., 28, 37, 39, 60, 63, 65, 101, 114, 130, 140
Anaximenes, 22 ff., 63, 65, 85, 175
Anima, 23
Animals, Parts of, 135, 162
Animals, History of, 135, 162
Animals, Coming-to-be of, 135, 162
Anti-particles, 42, 66
Antisthenes, 173, 175
Antony, Mark, 74, 173
Apollo – Delphi, 130
Apology, 85, 119
Approximations, 30-31
Apriorists, 35
Archimedes, 5, 179, 183
Archytas, 121
Aristarchus, 179
Aristophanes, 89
Aristotle, 1, 5, 6, 19, 22, 46, 48, 51, 56, 63, 65, 66, 69, 74, 90, 132 ff., 177, 182, 183, 186
Armstrong, A. H., 174
Arnold, Matthew, 52, 53
Art, 185, 186, 187; in Plato and Aristotle, 159
Asclepius, 93, 110, 133, 159
Assembly, Athenian, 77-79, 85, 89, 105
Astrology, 28, 176, 178, 180
Astronomy, 115, 165-6, 179-80
Athene, Pallas, 8, 9, 75, 106, 174
Athens, 73 ff., 135, 160, 169, 174, 179
Atlantic Ocean, 17, 179
Atom, 19, 50, 59, 64 ff., 102, 103, 140, 168, 178, 185
Atomic lengths, 48
Atomists, 56, 62 ff., 93, 100, 102, 186
Auden, W. H., 128
Augustus Caesar, 74, 176
Aurelius, Marcus, 176

Babylonia, 11, 12, 21, 25, 28, 30, 176
Banausoi-Banausic, 157, 182, 186
Beautiful, the, 91 ff., 96, 123, 173
Being, 44, 147
Biology, 135, 162
   Marine, 21, 133, 163
Bios – Bow and Life, 40
Blake, William, 6, 31, 122, 125, 184-5
Body, 33, 149
Booth, N. B., 48
Bowra, C. M., 117, 118
Breath – Fiery, 176
Brecht, 4
Bucephalus, 141, 142, 167

Categories, Aristotle's, 135-6
Causation, 66

Cause, in Aristotle, 138, 143-4, 146, 147, 168
Censorship, 128
Chamberlain, 42
Chance, 175
Change, 38, 46, 51, 53, 63, 127, 140 ff., 166
Chaos, 10, 11
Charmides, 121
Christianity, 7, 148, 170
Cicero, 134
Citizenship, 156-7
City State, 74, 120, 157, 168, 169, 174, 175, 182, 183
Classical Age, 74
Cleanthes, 180
Cleon, 77
Clerk-Maxwell, 50
Cockcroft, 69
Colombus, 179
Coming-to-be and Passing Away, 135, 146
Coming-to-be of Animals, 135, 162
Condensation, 22
Constitution of Athens, 135
Contemplation, 154-5, 157, 169
Continuum, 50
Contradiction, 6-7
Contraries, 146
Copleston, F. C., 170
Cornford, F. M., 165
Cosmogony, Hesiod's, 10; Anaximander's, 19; Plato-Timaeus, 100
Cosmology, Pythagorean, 26, 28-29
Cosmopolitanism, 175
Cosmos, 28, 37; of Atomists, 67; Aristotle's, 145, 166, 168
Council, Nocturnal, 129
Counter-earth, 29
Cratylus, 140
Creation, Plato-Timaeus, 100-1
Creator, 100, 148
Crete, 81, 127
Critias, 121, 177
Crito, 85, 119, 93
Cronos, 9, 11
Crossman, R. H. S., 118

Croton, 25, 26, 29
Crystals, 26, 56, 103
Cynics, 173-4

Dante, 171
Darwin, 22, 57, 66, 161, 166
Death, 177, 178
Decad, 29
De Interpretatione, 135
Delphi, 130
Delphic Oracle, 6, 86, 174
Democracy, Athenian, 78
Democritus, 56, 59, 62 ff., 73, 74, 102, 140, 166, 168, 171, 178, 185
Descartes, 50
Dialectic, 41, 46, 65, 87, 89, 95, 115, 125, 126, 136, 140, 155
Dichotomy, 46, 104, 182
Diogenes, 170, 172 ff.
Dionysius I, 121
Dionysius II, 173
Dionysus, 33, 34, 39
Divisibility, infinite, 46 ff.
Donne, 171
Drama, 159 ff., 186
Dualism, 33, 39

Earth, 21, 22, 26, 29, 35, 38, 52, 53, 101, 145-6, 167, 179-80 in Mythology, 10 ff.
Education, 4-5, 108 ff., 128, 156, 157
Egypt, 12 ff., 18, 21, 24, 25, 29, 30, 81, 104, 121, 127
Einstein, 2, 50, 139
Ekpurosis, 41
Elea and Eleatics, 43 ff., 50, 51, 53, 63, 65, 124
Elements, Four, 19 ff., 53, 54, 56, 101-2, 145, 146
Embryology, 162
Empedocles, 52 ff., 63, 65, 66, 68, 85, 101, 145, 168, 182, 186
Empiricism, 35, 45, 104, 179, 183
Ephesus, 36 ff.
Epicurus, 64 ff., 175, 177 ff., 185
Epimetheus, 105
Epistemology, 97

Er, 34
Eratosthenes, 179
Eros, 10, 11
Ether, 50, 67
Ethics, 73, 100, 135, 148, 151 ff., 169, 175, 178
Eugenics, 84, 113
Euripides, 58
Eurotas River, 80, 81, 126
Evolution, Theory of, in Anaximander, 21; in Empedocles, 56; opposition by Aristotle, 166 ff.
Experience, 99

Family, 155, 156
Faraday, 50
Fire, 20, 22, 29, 37 ff., 41, 42, 52, 53, 55, 56, 69, 102, 145, 146, 176, 186
Flux, 38, 98, 140
Form, 141 ff., 147, 148
Forms, Plato's, 91 ff., 100, 115, 119, 122 ff., 130, 131, 140, 142, 159, 165, 166
Freewill, 66
Freud, 161
Frost, Robert, 3

Gaia (Earth), 11
Galileo, 1, 4, 139, 166
Garden, the, 177, 178
Gassendi, 65
Geb, 12
Geometry, 13, 90, 95, 115, 184
Gizeh, Great Pyramid of, 13, 14
God, 29, 99, 100, 144, 147-8, 154, 157, 169, 176, 177
Golden Age, 126
Good, the, 87, 91, 93, 114, 115, 124, 125, 148, 151, 157, 177
Goodness, 86, 88, 96, 110, 115, 123, 125
Graves, Robert, 2
Gravitation, 57
Grene, Marjorie, 140
Guardians, 108 ff., 127, 177, 186
Gyges, 107

Happiness, 152 ff., 175
Hardy, Thomas, 187
Harmony, Laws of, 28-29, 40, 41
Hate, 53, 55, 56, 66
Heaven, 11, 56, 148, 175, 180, 186
Heavens, On the, 135
Hegel, 41
Hellenistic Age, 74, 172 ff.
Helots, 80, 82, 83, 160
Hephaestos, 8, 9, 106, 186
Heracleitus, 32, 36 ff., 44, 45, 49, 50, 60, 65, 66, 91, 98, 100, 114, 122, 130, 140, 141, 164, 165, 175, 176
Hero of Alexandria, 182
Herodotus, 12, 14, 76
Hesiod, 8, 10, 11, 12, 17, 39, 109, 128
Hippocratic Doctors and Medicine, 37, 162
History of Animals, 135
Homer, 8, 10, 11, 17, 24, 50, 63, 109, 128, 181; *Iliad* quoted 9; *Odyssey* quoted, 43
Hoyle, F., 139
Hubris, 187
Huxley, Aldous, 160
Huygens, 50
Hypotenuse, 14, 29, 30

Idealism, 91, 178, 182
Ideas, Plato's, 91 ff., 115, 124 ff.
Indeterminate Swerve, 67, 70, 178
Ionians, 17 ff., 35, 37, 61, 65, 76, 81, 91, 114; Rationalist Movement, 10, 15
Iris (Rainbow), Daughter of Thaumas (Wonder), 186
Iron, 183
Irrational Number, 29, 30

Jeans, Sir James, 58
Jowett, Benjamin, 126, 185
Jung, 41
Justice, 27, 28, 86, 88, 91, 106 ff., 110, 115, 123, 126; Cosmic, 20, 28, 114

Kepler, 26, 166

Knowledge, 87, 95 ff., 139, 140, 143, 152, 178, 185

Law, Natural, 66, 67, 85,
Laws, 90, 119, 123, 127 ff., 159
Lee, H. D. P., 47
Leisure, 155, 157, 169
Lesbos, 77, 133
Leucippus, 59, 63 ff., 71
Light, 54, 55, 68
Locke, John, 116, 184, 185
Logic, 44, 45, 50, 63, 134 ff., 170, 171
Love, 53, 55, 56, 66,
Lucretius, 59, 60, 64, 67, 70, 178
Lyceum, 65, 90, 134, 163, 177, 179
Lycurgus, 80 ff., 109, 126
Lyre, 25, 28

Macedon, 133, 134, 169, 174, 176, 177
MacNeice, L., 97
Magnet, 60
Man, 137, 143, 149, 152, 155, 160, 164, 167
Marduk, 12, 18
Marx, 41
Mathematicians, Council of, 123
Mathematics, 71, 115, 173, 179, 181, 182, 184
Matter, 67, 71, 101, 141, 142, 146, 147, 148, 182, 184
Mean, Aristotelian, 153, 158; Arithmetic and Harmonic, 28
Measurement, 15, 71, 139
Medicine, 52, 159, 162, 179
Melos, 78, 86
Meno, 87, 94
Metaphysics, 135, 147, 154
Metempsychosis, 35
Meteorologica, 135
Middle Term, 138
Miletus and Milesians, 17, 19, 25, 35, 37, 58, 63, 76, 78, 86
Mind (Nous), 60, 70, 85, 178, 183
Modes, Dorian, Ionian and Lydian, 109
Monism and Monistic Theory, 49, 65, 71, 124

Moon, 1, 29, 56, 58, 60, 61, 138, 145, 166, 167
Motion (Movement), 45-46, 51, 70, 140, 141, 144 ff.
Mover, Prime, 147-8
Muses, 4, 90
Music, 28, 109, 127, 160
  of the Spheres, 29, 114
Myth, 9; of the Cave, 92
Mytilene, 77-78, 86, 133

Nature, 140, 142, 144, 155, 157, 163, 164, 166 ff., 184
Newton, 3, 65, 139, 166, 184, 185
Nicomachean Ethics, 135
Nile, 13 ff., 104
Northrop, E. P., 51
Number, 27 ff.; Irrational, 115; Theory of, 167
Nun (Primeval Ocean), 14, 18
Nut (Sky goddess), 12

Odysseus, 34, 82, 89, 154; and *Odyssey* quoted 43
Oedipus at Colonus, 75, 129
Okeanos, 12
Olympia, 35, 143, 179
Olympus, 8, 9, 10, 17, 23, 186
Opposites, 39 ff., 45, 146
Organon, 135, 136, 168
Orpheus, 32 ff., 177
Orphism, 33 ff., 39, 53, 92, 106
Ovid, 87

Paradoxes, 6, 7, 46 ff., 59; Plato's, 116; Plato – a paradox, 117
Parmenides, 44 ff., 53, 58, 63, 64, 65, 91, 119, 123, 124, 125, 140, 141, 165, 175, 186
Particles, 42, 55, 59, 65, 71; Alpha, 68; Discrete, 46
Passing Away and Coming-to-be, 135, 146
Peloponnesian War, 77, 79, 120
Pericles, 58, 77, 78, 79, 85, 98, 105, 120

Peripatetics, 134
Phaedo, 61, 85, 93, 100, 119
Phaedrus, 119, 125
Phainarete (and Socrates as midwife), 99
Pharaohs, 13 ff.
Phidias, 143
Philip of Macedon, 133
Philosopher-Kings, 129, 133
Phoenicians, 17, 176
Physics, 71, 100, 147, 165, 178, 182; Aristotle's, 135: Nuclear, 57
Planets, 29, 56, 145
Plato, 1, 5, 7, 27, 33 ff., 41, 48, 61, 62, 65, 66, 73, 74, 85, 89, 90 ff., 132 ff., 140, 142, 143, 146, 149, 156, 157, 159, 160, 162, 165, 166, 173, 174, 177, 179, 182, 184, 185, 186
Plenum, 44, 50, 65
Pluralism and Pluralists, 63, 65, 71, 124
Plutarch, 47, 81, 82, 83, 173, 183
Poetics, 135, 159-60
Politics, 135, 144, 155 ff., 167, 168, 169, 173
Polycrates, Tyrant of Samos, 25, 26
Pope, Alexander, 4; Essay on Criticism, 6; Moral Essays, 71
Popper, Karl, 42, 102, 103, 118, 165
Pores, 54 ff.
Poseidon, 9, 10, 11, 43, 75, 122, 128
Potential, 49, 141, 142, 147, 166
Pound, Ezra, 97
Predicables, 137
Prometheus, 105, 106, 186
Protagoras, 100, 101, 131; Plato's, 98, 99, 105
Psyche, 41; as Breath, Soul, 23
Psychology, 135, 154, 186, 187
Ptolemies, 50, 179
Purgation, of Emotions (Pity, Fear, etc.), 160
Pyramids: Great Pyramid of Gizeh, 13 ff.; Great Pyramid, 18; Perfect Pyramid, 26

Pythagoras and Pythagoreans, 5, 25 ff., 32 ff., 39, 44, 50, 53, 65, 88, 91, 92, 102, 103, 104, 121, 135, 140, 149, 165, 167, 177

Quintessence, 146
Quintilian, 134

Rarefaction, 22
Reason, 27, 45, 51, 100, 101, 149, 176, 185
Refutations, Sophistic, 135, 136
Reincarnation, 34, 53
Republic, 34, 90, 92, 105 ff., 118, 119, 122, 123, 125 ff., 159, 184
Rhetoric, 135, 179
Rome, 6, 176
Rope-Knotters (Egyptian), 13, 15
Russell, Bertrand, 118, 171
Rutherford, 68, 69

Saint-Exupéry, 181
Saint Paul, 82, 87
Sambursky, S., 30, 31, 57
Samos, 25, 26, 177, 179
Sartre, 181
Scepticism, 7
Science, 37, 147, 181, 182, 184
Seeds, 59, 65, 67
Segré, 42
Seltman, 26
Senses, 24, 37, 49, 50, 57, 68, 91, 95 ff., 115, 140, 164, 178, 185, 186
Sequence, Tragic, 187
Shakespeare, 32, 63, 74, 112, 171
Shu, 12
Shuttle, Automatic, 170, 183
Sicily, 52, 173
Simeon, 35
Simmias, 95 ff.
Simonides, 83
Slavery and Slaves, 182, 183; in Aristotle, 155-6, 168 ff.
Snell, 50
Socrates, 6, 7, 41, 61, 73 ff., 85 ff., 90 ff., 105 ff., 119, 121, 124, 125, 129, 136, 159, 170, 173, 175, 179, 182, 183, 184

Solids, Geometric, 26, 27, 102, 103
Soma-Sema, 33
Sophists, 86, 98, 136
Sophocles, 58, 75, 129, 130, 174
Soul, 33, 70, 92ff., 109, 115, 135, 140,
    148ff., 152, 153, 155, 164, 177,
    178
Space (*see also* Void and Vacuum),
    63, 64, 148, 178
Sparta, 80ff., 86, 109, 127, 156, 157,
    160
Species, 165, 166
Sphere, Perfect, 26, 35
Spheres, 145, 146, 148, 155
    Music of, 29, 114
Stagira, 133
State, 155, 156, 158, 177
Statesman, 126
Stoa, 175, 178
Stoics, 41, 175ff.
Strife, 40, 41
Substance, 136, 137, 141, 144, 145,
    147
Sun, 12, 18, 56, 58, 60, 61, 68, 138,
    146, 147, 166, 167, 172; centre
    of earth's orbit, 180
Swerve, Indeterminate, 67, 70, 178
Syllogism, 137, 138
Symposium, 119
Syracuse, 121, 173, 183

Tacitus, 7
Teleology, 73, 101, 144, 165, 180
Tennyson, 144, 166
Tension, of Contraries, 40, 41
Thales, 5, 18ff., 25, 37, 60, 63, 65,
    179, 182
Theaetetus, 97ff., 185
Theatre, 160, 161
Themis, 9, 10
Theogony, 10, 11
Theology, 73, 147
Theorem, 35
Thomson, J. A. K., 132
Thrasymachus, 106, 107
Thucydides, 77, 78, 120
Tiamat, 12

Timaeus, 100, 101, 125, 146
Time, 129, 130, 148
Titans, 11, 12, 13, 186
Topics, 135
Tragedies, Dramatic, 160, 187
Transmigration of Souls, 149
Triangles, 29, 30, 102ff., 146
Twain, Mark, 4
Typhoeus, 11, 12
Truth (and the True), 86, 87, 88, 91,
    95, 110, 119, 123, 148, 159, 173

Universals, 119, 138
Universe, 139; Aristotle's, 145ff.,
    168; and the Stoics, 176; and
    Epicurus, 178; non-geocentric,
    of Aristarchus, 180, 181

Vacuum (*see also* Space and Void),
    58, 68
Virologists (and Geometric Shapes),
    103
Virtue, 87, 94, 98, 152, 153, 154, 173
Void (*see also* Space and Vacuum),
    44, 46, 50, 69, 140, 148, 178
Vortex, 56, 60, 66

Walton, 69
War (in Heracleitus' scheme), 40, 41
Water, 12, 18ff., 53, 54, 55, 70, 101,
    102, 145, 146
Wave-Particle Duality, 71
Wheel of Birth, 34
Whitehead, A. N., 182
Wilson, J. A., 12, 15
Wisdom, 2, 4, 97, 122, 138
Wonder (origin of Philosophy), 139
Wordsworth, 93

Xenocrates, 48
Xenophanes, 24

Yeats, W. B., 3, 5, 71, 130, 131

Zeno, of Citium, 175, 176
Zeno, of Elea, 7, 45ff., 53, 59, 91,
    124, 135, 141
Zeus, 8ff., 33, 41, 74, 106, 143, 173,
    186